An Apache Campaign in the Sierra Madre

CRAWFORD'S COLUMN MOVING TO THE FRONT.

AN APACHE CAMPAIGN IN THE SIERRA MADRE

AN ACCOUNT OF THE EXPEDITION IN PURSUIT OF THE
HOSTILE CHIRICAHUA APACHES IN THE
SPRING OF 1883.

BY
JOHN G. BOURKE

Foreword by Joseph C. Porter

ILLUSTRATED

University of Nebraska Press
Lincoln and London

Foreword copyright © 1987 by the
University of Nebraska Press
Manufactured in the United States of America

First Bison Book printing: 1987
Most recent printing indicated by the first digit below:
1   2   3   4   5   6   7   8   9   10

Library of Congress Cataloging-in-Publication Data
Bourke, John Gregory, 1846–1896.
  An Apache Campaign in the Sierra Madre.
  Reprint. Originally published: New York: Scribner,
1886. With new foreword.
  "Bison book"—T.p. verso
  1. Apache Indians—Wars, 1883–1886. I. Title.
E83.88.B76 1987   973.8′4   87-5940
ISBN 0-9032-6085-7 (pbk.)

Reprinted from the 1886 edition published by
Charles Scribner's Sons

The University of Nebraska Press acknowledges with
appreciation the loan of a copy of the book for reproduction
from the Christlieb Collection, Center for Great Plains
Studies, University of Nebraska–Lincoln.

FOREWORD
by Joseph C. Porter

An Apache Campaign was first published in February 1886 and quickly became a classic in western American writing as well as a key source in frontier military history. It is a stirring adventure narrative relating Brigadier General George Crook's daring military foray into the Sierra Madre of Mexico, where he overtook the unsuspecting Chiricahua Apaches.

Unorthodox behavior typified the career of George Crook (1828–90) as an Indian fighter, and never more so than during his Sierra Madre campaign. A prominent Union officer during the Civil War, Crook had successfully fought Indians in the Pacific Northwest and, during the early 1870s, in Arizona. He was a pivotal figure in the Great Sioux War of 1876. A deteriorating situation in the Apache homeland prompted the army to order Crook to Arizona in 1882. Fragmented bands of Chihenne, Bedonkohe, Chokonen, and Nednai Apaches—collectively known as Chiricahuas—hid in the mountains of Mexico. From their remote sanctuaries, the

Chiricahuas raided Mexican farms and ranches, and they remained a constant threat to Crook's efforts to stabilize the situation in Arizona.

Experience against the Western Apaches in the 1870s had convinced Crook that it was futile to rely solely upon soldiers to fight them. He was certain that only Apaches were capable of subduing their hostile brethren, and he began enlisting large numbers of Apache auxiliaries. By 1873 Crook's experiment brought a tenuous peace to Arizona. A decade later Crook turned to his old methods to root the Chiricahuas from their Sierra Madre hideouts. In the spring of 1883 Crook enlisted 193 Western Apache scouts. With his Apache army and less than fifty soldiers, Crook severed all communications and led his force into Mexico.

John Gregory Bourke had served on Crook's staff since 1871, and he had fought against the hostile Western Apaches in the early 1870s and against the Teton Sioux and Northern Cheyennes in 1876. By 1883 Bourke had earned a reputation as a skilled ethnologist and folklorist, as well as respect for his accomplishments as a combat officer. During the Sierra Madre expedition Bourke served as one of Crook's key liaisons with the Apache scouts.

Bourke believed that the Chiricahuas were the most formidable opponents that Crook had faced. In his opinion, several factors made them especially dangerous. He noted the stamina and physical endurance of the Chiricahua renegades and their Western Apache cousins. He was aware of the Chiricahuas' determined resignation to die fighting. Chiricahua contact with Americans and Mexicans had been violent and brutal. One token of their resignation was the fact that, by 1883, the Chiricahuas referred to themselves as "*Indeh*" or "the Dead."*

Bourke also observed that the Chiricahua leaders were very intelligent and quite courageous. All of their headmen—Geronimo, Loco, Nana, Bonito, Chihuahua, Chato, Ulzana, Mangus, Zele, and Kayatennae—were, Bourke wrote, "men of noticeable brain power, power, physically perfect, and mentally acute—just the individuals to lead a forlorn hope in the face of every obstacle." Throughout this campaign, Crook had to match wits continually against men of obvious ability.

Events rewarded Crook's trust in his Apache scouts. Despite the mountainous terrain and the wariness of their opponents, the Apache scouts

---

*The Apache term *Indah* means "The Living" and *Indeh* means "The Dead." The latter "is the term by which Apaches, recognizing their fate, designated themselves." Eve Ball, *Indeh: An Apache Odyssey,* (Provo, Utah: Brigham Young University Press, 1980), xix, 76–77.

found the Chiricahua sanctuaries in the Sierra Madre. Moreover, they reached the Chiricahua hideouts undetected. One sharp skirmish ensued between Crook's Apache scouts and the Chiricahuas, and then Crook opened negotiations. Adopting a pose of belligerant confidence, Crook proceeded by discussion rather than by force.

This became Crook's finest hour as an Indian fighting army officer. His accomplishment during the volatile days that followed cannot be overlooked. The situation was extremely dangerous. Backed only by his Apache scouts, Crook faced a potentially desperate adversary. He was in a foreign country and miles from his own border. Given their past history with the Anglos, the Chiricahuas had no reason to believe Crook. Yet the general acted as if he controlled events. Simultaneously, he bluffed and cajoled the wary Chiricahua headmen, earning the trust of some of them. "Had Geronimo actually opted for war, all would have been lost, and Crook knew it," historian Dan Thrapp has written. "He bid high on a hole card that was blank, but he put it over." Incredibly, Crook *talked* Geronimo and the Chiricahuas into returning peacefully to Arizona.

An Apache Campaign depicts Crook's success in Mexico, but Bourke intended his book to be more than a narrative of the expedition. It was a spirited defense of the Apache peoples, and it excoriated government Indian policy that (in Bourke's opinion) had shamefully betrayed the Apaches. Bourke's explicit critique of previous Indian policy was an effort to espouse implicitly Crook's and his own particular approach to Indian policy. Bourke and Crook believed that the Apaches should become self-supporting and govern themselves as much as possible on their reservations.

Bourke wrote about Apache cultures and individuals with openmindedness and candor. These qualities made *An Apache Campaign* especially remarkable in an era when bombastic and bloodcurdling newspaper articles described the Apaches as fiends. Indeed, at that time the *Tombstone Epitaph* was advising its readership on how to get away with murdering peaceful Apaches. *An Apache Campaign* recounts the history of corruption and lies that had convinced the Chiricahuas to go on the warpath. For Bourke, the real foe was not the Chiricahuas but Anglo and Hispanic settlers and politicians who coveted Indian lands and bedeviled the Apaches. Bourke also censured the "Indian rings" of corrupt Indian agents and their cohorts who cheated the Apaches out of their annuity goods.

Bourke's background made him an effective

advocate for Indian rights. He was not a bleed-
ing-heart greenhorn pontificating about the
"noble savage." Rather, he was a cavalry veter-
an who had fought against several tribes in the
Southwest and on the Great Plains. His bat-
tlefield experience led him to study the cultures
of his former enemies, and the more that he
learned about Indians the more he came to
empathize with their plight. He developed an
especially close relationship with the Western
Apaches and the Chiricahuas. *An Apache Campaign* reveals Bourke's sympathies when he
heaps sarcasm upon groups like the "Tombstone
Rangers," or when he derides futile Mexican
efforts to conquer the Chiricahuas.

At first glance, *An Apache Campaign* recounts Crook's military adventure in Mexico
and introduces readers to the Apaches. In *An
Apache Campaign* Bourke captured a brief, confident moment in the violent history of Apacheria. Peaceful negotiations had succeeded in the
Sierra Madre. The Chiricahuas, true to their
word, eventually did return to Arizona, where it
seemed that Crook and Bourke could implement
their own Indian policy. For an instant it
appeared that Crook had pacified the Chiricahuas, confounded his enemies within the Indian
Bureau, and brought peace to Arizona. *An
Apache Campaign* ends on this confident note.

On 10 June 1882, Crook and 384 Chiricahuas crossed the border into Arizona. The Sierra Madre adventure was over, and here Bourke ended *An Apache Campaign*. Essentially, *An Apache Campaign* accurately tells of Crook's venture, but the story of the book itself does not end here.

Within days of Crook's return to the United States, critics of his policy threatened to destroy his accomplishments in Mexico. Arizonians clamored for the arrest and trial of the more notorious Chiricahua leaders. This alarmed the always wary Chiricahuas, and it broke Crook's assurances made to them in the Sierra Madre. Then the civilian Indian agent initially refused to accept the Chiricahua warriors at the San Carlos Reservation.

Critics soon accused Crook of lying about the Sierra Madre campaign. Rumors spread that Crook had not caught the Chiricahuas, but that Geronimo had captured Crook and his men, who were lucky to have escaped with their lives. Others charged that Crook's trusted Apache scouts had actually sided with the renegade Chiricahuas. Many Arizonans and some officials in Washington were dumbfounded that Crook had consented to let some of the Chiricahuas return on their own to Arizona. It was rumored that Geronimo spared Crook's command only after the frightened and cornered general acquiesced to the Chiricahuas' demands.

The controversy intensified during the summer and autumn of 1883. Critics, especially those in Arizona, simply could not comprehend Crook's behavior toward the Apaches. Years of Apache warfare with attendant violence had left a potent legacy of racial hatred in the Southwest, and many could not comprehend why an American general acepted the work of "bronco" Apaches. Some sincerely believed that Geronimo must have captured Crook because that alone explained his apparently irrational conduct and that was also why the general had not exterminated the hostiles but merely had returned to Arizona with more than three hundred Chiricahuas and still more on the way. Most Arizonans would have preferred that Crook had annihilated the Chiricahuas in Mexico. They wanted less, not more, Apaches in Arizona.

The furor increased because some of the Chiricahuas lingered in Mexico. In the Sierra Madre in 1883, the headmen assured Crook that they hoped to cross the border in about sixty days, but three months passed with no word from them. During the autumn of 1883, Naiche, Zele, and their bands returned to Arizona, and in February of 1884 Mangus and Chato finally reached the border. In March 1884, Geronimo arrived in

Arizona, and in May a few more Chiricahua stragglers crossed the border. Finally, a full year after the Sierra Madre expedition, all of the Chiricahuas were at San Carlos Reservation. Crook ordered them north to Turkey Creek near Fort Apache. Here Crook and Bourke attempted to implement their Apache policy.

While Crook awaited the Chiricahuas, the government of Mexico complained that the Chiricahuas in Mexico were still raiding Mexican farms and ranches. The Indian Bureau and Crook feuded over who would control the Chiricahuas on the reservation. Bourke alleged that the "Indian rings" were determined to undermine Crook's goal of making the Apaches self-sufficient. Territorial newspapers flailed Crook in their pages.

This atmosphere of lies, rumors, and doubts motivated Bourke to write a series of articles about the Sierra Madre campaign. Based on Bourke's diary, the articles became the book *An Apache Campaign.* The context within which Bourke prepared his manuscript explains its confident, buoyant tone, and it underscores Bourke's role as unofficial press agent for Crook, a function he had performed since joining the general's staff in 1871.

In 1883 and 1884 Bourke wrote his articles defending Crook and the Western Apache scouts

and explaining the Chiricahua point of view.
Bourke's diary and *An Apache Campaign* agree
on matters of fact, but there is a profound difference in tone and emphasis between the two.
Bourke intended *An Apache Campaign* to refute
the ridiculous accusations against Crook and
the Western Apache scouts. The book proclaims
that success was a foregone conclusion once
Geronimo arrived at Crook's camp. Further-
more, *An Apache Campaign* insists that Crook's
stern pose easily convinced Geronimo and the
other Chiricahua headmen to return to Arizona.

Bourke's diary, on the other hand, reveals
that the situation in the Sierra Madre remained
volatile and dangerous. The diary and the
narrative of John Rope, a Western Apache scout,
clearly indicate that nothing was assured until
the Chiricahuas actually arrived in Arizona.
Reading the diary or Rope's account only en-
hances one's respect for the enormity of Crook's
gamble and for his accomplishment.

Publication of *An Apache Campaign* in 1886
marked a significant step for Bourke as a writer.
In 1884 Charles Scribner's Sons had published
Bourke's *The Snake Dance of the Moquis of Arizona* to glowing reviews in the United States
and Europe. This book had established Bourke
as a prominent ethnologist and as a vivid and descriptive anthropological writer. Additional ar-

ticles enhanced his stature as a scientist, and in 1885 he became a member of the American Association for the Advancement of Science.

His *Outing Magazine* articles, which resulted in the book-length *An Apache Campaign,* broadened Bourke's reputation and established him as a popular writer about western topics and military history. Bourke enjoyed great success with *An Apache Campaign,* and both book and magazine publishers now sought manuscripts from him. After 1886 the reading public accepted Bourke as a scientific and popular writer on anthropological and general western topics.

An Apache Campaign presaged Bourke's monumental classic, *On the Border with Crook,* published by Scribner's in 1891. His vivid style was evident in both books. Bourke skillfully described terrain and landscape, bringing his readers directly into the mountain and desert environment of Apacheria. Readers huff, puff, and sweat along with Bourke and the exhausted soldiers as they climb the treacherous sierras. Readers more fully appreciate the Apache scouts who cover the same ground so effortlessly. After recreating the locale, Bourke populates it with interesting and authentic characters. Readers see a new picture of the Apaches because Bourke pierces ethnocentric stereotypes and biases to depict Apache cultures and distinct individuals within those cultures. He denounces those who perverted and corrupted government Indian policy.

For Bourke the writer, *An Apache Campaign* was a success. Yet Bourke's hopes for the Chiricahuas were dead before the book actually appeared in 1886. Crook's enemies within the Indian Bureau and in Arizona prevented him from keeping his promises to the Chiricahuas. Disillusioned, a faction of the Chiricahuas headed by Geronimo fled the reservation in May 1885. More than three hundred Chiricahuas stayed at Turkey Creek, dutifully keeping their word to Crook. Indeed, some Chiricahua warriors served the army as scouts in hunting for Geronimo. Geronimo's *émeute* entirely discredited Crook, and the chieftain's actions had disastrous consequences for all of the Chiricahuas.

Crook lost the confidence of his superiors; one rival general, Nelson A. Miles, schemed to replace him in Arizona. Failure haunted Crook's efforts to capture the elusive Geronimo. In March 1886 (one month after *An Apache Campaign* appeared) members of the "Indian ring" sabotaged a shaky truce between Crook and Geronimo. Geronimo again escaped, and Crook resigned his command in Arizona. Bourke's literary accomplishments earned him a five-year stint in Washington, D.C. writing treatises on anthropology and folklore. Crook's successor in Arizona, Brigadier General Nelson A. Miles, eventually banished the entire Chiricahua tribe to prisoner-of-war camps in Florida.

An Apache Campaign is a clear-eyed narrative of Crook's finest achievement as an Indian fighter. It expresses the fleeting hope that Crook (and Bourke) could somehow undo the damage of years of corrupt Indian management. For a moment in 1883, Bourke envisioned the peoples of the Southwest — Anglo, Hispanic, and Indian — enjoying productive and peaceful lives. The fleeting but genuine success in the Sierra Madre inspired Bourke's hopes for an enduring peace with the Chiricahuas. Today, a century later, *An Apache Campaign* recaptures those pivotal days in the Sierra Madre when it seemed possible to open a new era in Apacheria. A good tale and a first-class history, *An Apache Campaign* is also a monument to the aspirations of George Crook and John Gregory Bourke.

Postscript: At the end of *An Apache Campaign* Bourke notes that the army officers of his time never learned the fate of little Charlie McComas. In 1959 an elderly Bedonkohe, Jason Betzinez, once a member of Geronimo's band, finally revealed the truth. In the initial skirmish, Captain Emmett Crawford and the Western Apache scouts attacked the Chiricahua camp, and during the fight some of the scouts killed an old woman. Enraged at the death of his mother, a Chiricahua man crushed Charlie McComas's head with a rock and threw the body into the brush. The Chiricahuas sternly disapproved of killing the captive child, but fearing retribution, they feigned ignorance.

Sources

For John G. Bourke, consult Joseph C. Porter, *Paper Medicine Man: John Gregory Bourke and His American West* (1986). This book deals in depth with Bourke's relationship with George Crook and the Sierra Madre campaign. For General George Crook, see John Gregory Bourke, *On the Border with Crook* (1891) and Martin F. Schmitt, ed., *General George Crook: His Autobiography* (1986). For an excellent analysis of the campaign, see Dan L. Thrapp, *General Crook and the Sierra Madre Adventure* (1972). Thrapp's *The Conquest of Apacheria* (1967) is an essential history of the Apache wars.

Several works examine the Chiricahua perspective. Angie Debo's *Geronimo: The Man, His Time, His Place* (1976) treats the noted Apache shaman. Eve Ball compiled two excellent narratives: *Indeh: An Apache Odyssey* (1980) and *In the Days of Victor-*

io: Recollections of a Warm Springs Apache (1970). Another useful source is Jason Betzinez, with W. S. Nye, *I Fought with Geronimo* (1959).

For the point of view of one of Crook's Western Apache scouts, see the fascinating account of John Rope in Keith Basso, ed., *Western Apache Raiding and Warfare* (1971). Also, consult the narrative of former Apache scout David Longstreet in this same volume.

PREFACE.

The recent outbreak of a fraction of the Chiricahua Apaches, and the frightful atrocities which have marked their trail through Arizona, Sonora, New Mexico, and Chihuahua, has attracted renewed attention to these brave but bloodthirsty aborigines and to the country exposed to their ravages.

The contents of this book, which originally appeared in a serial form in the *Outing Magazine* of Boston, represent the details of the expedition led by General Crook to the Sierra Madre, Mexico, in 1883; but, as the present military operations are conducted by the same commander, against the same enemy, and upon the same field of action, a perusal of these pages will, it is confidently believed, place before the reader a better knowledge of the general situation than any article which is likely soon to appear.

There is this difference to be noted, however; of the one hundred and twenty-five (125) fighting men brought back from the Sierra Madre, less than one-third have engaged in the present hostilities, from which fact an additional inference may be drawn both of the difficulties to be overcome in the repression of these disturbances and of the horrors which would surely have accumulated upon the heads of our citizens had the *whole* fighting force of this fierce band taken to the mountains.

One small party of eleven (11) hostile Chiricahuas, during the period from November 15th, 1885, to the present date, has killed twenty-one (21) friendly Apaches living in peace upon the reservation, and no less than twenty-five (25) white men, women, and children. This bloody raid has been conducted through a country filled with regular troops, militia, and "rangers," —and at a loss to the enemy, so far as can be shown, of only one man, whose head is now at Fort Apache.

JOHN G. BOURKE.

Apache Indian Agency,
San Carlos, Arizona,
December 15th, 1885.

LIST OF ILLUSTRATIONS.

AN APACHE CAMPAIGN.

I.

WITHIN the compass of this volume it is impossible to furnish a complete dissertation upon the Apache Indians or the causes which led up to the expedition about to be described. The object is simply to outline some of the difficulties attending the solution of the Indian question in the South-west and to make known the methods employed in conducting campaigns against savages in hostility. It is thought that the object desired can best be accomplished by submitting an unmutilated extract from the journal carefully kept during the whole period involved.

Much has necessarily been excluded, but without exception it has been to avoid repetition, or else to escape the introduction of information bearing upon the language, the religion, marriages, funeral ceremonies, etc., of this interesting race, which would increase the bulk of the manuscript, and, perhaps, detract from its value in the eyes of the general reader.

Ethnologically the Apache is classed with the Tinneh tribes, living close to the Yukon and Mackenzie rivers, within the Arctic circle. For centuries he has been preëminent over the more peaceful nations about him for courage, skill, and daring in war; cunning in deceiving and evading his enemies; ferocity in attack when skilfully-planned ambuscades have led an unwary foe into his clutches; cruelty and brutality to captives; patient endurance and fortitude under the greatest privations.

In peace he has commanded respect for keen-sighted intelligence, good fellowship, warmth of feeling for his friends, and impatience of wrong.

No Indian has more virtues and none has been more truly ferocious when aroused. He was the first of the native Americans to defeat in battle or outwit in diplomacy the all-conquering, smooth-tongued Spaniard, with whom and his Mexican-mongrel descendants he has

waged cold-blooded, heart-sickening war since
the days of Cortés. When the Spaniard had
fire-arms and corselet of steel he was unable to
push back this fierce, astute aborigine, provided
simply with lance and bow. The past fifty
years have seen the Apache provided with
arms of precision, and, especially since the introduction of magazine breech-loaders, the
Mexican has not only ceased to be an intruder
upon the Apache, but has trembled for the
security of life and property in the squalid
hamlets of the States of Chihuahua and Sonora.

In 1871 the War Department confided to
General George Crook the task of whipping
into submission all the bands of the Apache
nation living in Arizona. How thoroughly
that duty was accomplished is now a matter of
history. But at the last moment one band—
the Chiricahuas—was especially exempted from
Crook's jurisdiction. They were not attacked
by troops, and for years led a Jack-in-the-box
sort of an existence, now popping into an
agency and now popping out, anxious, if their
own story is to be credited, to live at peace

with the whites, but unable to do so from lack of nourishment.

When they went upon the reservation, rations in abundance were promised for themselves and families. A difference of opinion soon arose with the agent as to what constituted a ration, the wicked Indians laboring under the delusion that it was enough food to keep the recipient from starving to death, and objecting to an issue of supplies based upon the principle according to which grumbling Jack-tars used to say that prize-money was formerly apportioned,—that is, by being thrown through the rungs of a ladder—what stuck being the share of the Indian, and what fell to the ground being the share of the agent. To the credit of the agent it must be said that he made a praiseworthy but ineffectual effort to alleviate the pangs of hunger by a liberal distribution of hymn-books among his wards. The perverse Chiricahuas, not being able to digest works of that nature, and unwilling to acknowledge the correctness of the agent's arithmetic, made up their minds to sally out from San Carlos and take refuge in the more hospitable wilderness of the Sierra Madre. Their discontent was not allayed by rumors whispered about of the intention of the agent to have the whole tribe removed bodily to the Indian Territory. Coal had been discovered on the reservation, and speculators clamored that the land involved be thrown open for development, regardless of the rights of the Indians. But, so the story goes, matters suddenly reached a focus when the agent one day sent his chief of police to arrest a Chiricahua charged with some offense deemed worthy of punishment in the guard-house. The offender started to run through the Indian camp, and the chief of police fired at him, but missed his aim and killed a luckless old squaw, who happened in range. This wretched marksmanship was resented by the Chiricahuas, who refused to be comforted by the profuse apologies tendered for the accident. They silently made their preparations, waiting long enough to catch the chief of police, kill him, cut off his head, and play a game of foot-ball with it; and then, like a flock of quail, the whole band, men, women, and children—710 in all—started on the dead run for

the Mexican boundary, one hundred and fifty
miles to the south.

Hotly pursued by the troops, they fought
their way across Southern Arizona and New
Mexico, their route marked by blood and dev-
astation. The valleys of the Santa Cruz and
San Pedro witnessed a repetition of the once
familiar scenes of farmers tilling their fields
with rifles and shot-guns strapped to the plow-
handle. While engaged in fighting off the
American forces, which pressed too closely upon
their rear, the Apaches were attacked in front
by the Mexican column under Colonel Garcia,
who, in a savagely contested fight, achieved a
"substantial victory," killing eighty-five and
capturing thirty, eleven of which total of one
hundred and fifteen were men, and the rest
women and children. The Chiricahuas claim
that when the main body of their warriors
reached the scene of the engagement the Mexicans evinced no anxiety to come out from the
rifle-pits they hastily dug. To this fact no
allusion can be found in the Mexican commander's published dispatches.

The Chiricahuas, now reduced to an aggre-

APACHE VILLAGE SCENE.

gate of less than 600—150 of whom were warriors and big boys, withdrew to the recesses
of the adjacent Sierra Madre—their objective
point. Not long after this the Chiricahuas
made overtures for an armistice with the Mexicans, who invited them to a little town near
Casas Grandes, Chihuahua, for a conference.
They were courteously received, plied with
liquor until drunk, and then attacked tooth and
nail, ten or twelve warriors being killed and
some twenty-five or thirty women hurried off
to captivity.

This is a one-sided description of the affair,
given by a Chiricahua who participated. The
newspapers of that date contained telegraph accounts of a fierce battle and another "victory"
from Mexican sources; so that no doubt there
is some basis for the story.

Meantime General Crook had been reassigned
by the President to the command of the Department of Arizona, which he had left nearly
ten years previously in a condition of peace and
prosperity, with the Apaches hard at work
upon the reservation, striving to gain a living
by cultivating the soil. Incompetency and

rascality, in the interval, had done their worst,
and when Crook returned not only were the
Chiricahuas on the war-path, but all the other
bands of the Apache nation were in a state
of scarcely concealed defection and hostility.
Crook lost not a moment in visiting his old
friends among the chiefs and warriors, and by
the exercise of a strong personal influence,
coupled with assurances that the wrongs of
which the Apaches complained should be
promptly redressed, succeeded in averting an
outbreak which would have made blood flow
from the Pecos to the Colorado, and for the
suppression of which the gentle and genial tax-
payer would have been compelled to contribute
most liberally of his affluence. Attended by
an aid-de-camp, a surgeon, and a dozen Apache
scouts, General Crook next proceeded to the
south-east corner of Arizona, from which point
he made an attempt to open up communication
with the Chiricahuas. In this he was unsuc-
cessful, but learned from a couple of squaws,
intercepted while attempting to return to the
San Carlos, that the Chiricahuas had sworn ven-
geance upon Mexicans and Americans alike;

that their stronghold was an impregnable position in the Sierra Madre, a "great way" below the International Boundary; and that they supplied themselves with an abundance of food by raiding upon the cattle-ranches and "haciendas" in the valleys and plains below.

Crook now found himself face to face with the following intricate problem : The Chiricahuas occupied a confessedly impregnable position in the precipitous range known as the Sierra Madre. This position was within the territory of another nation so jealous of its privileges as not always to be able to see clearly in what direction its best interests lay. The territory harassed by the Chiricahuas not only stretched across the boundary separating Mexico from the United States, but was divided into four military departments—two in each country; hence an interminable amount of jealousy, suspicion, fault-finding, and antagonism would surely dog the steps of him who should endeavor to bring the problem to a solution.

To complicate matters further, the Chiricahuas, and all the other Apaches as well, were filled with the notion that the Mexicans were a horde of cowards and treacherous liars, afraid to meet them in war but valiant enough to destroy their women and children, for whose blood, by the savage's law of retaliation, blood must in turn be shed. Affairs went on in this unsatisfactory course from October, 1882, until March, 1883, everybody in Arizona expecting a return of the dreaded Chiricahuas, but no one knowing where the first attack should be made. The meagre military force allotted to the department was distributed so as to cover as many exposed points as possible, one body of 150 Apache scouts, under Captain Emmet Crawford, Third Cavalry, being assigned to the arduous duty of patrolling the Mexican boundary for a distance of two hundred miles, through a rugged country pierced with ravines and cañons. No one was suprised to learn that toward the end of March this skeleton line had been stealthily penetrated by a bold band of twenty-six Chiricahuas, under a very crafty and daring young chief named *Chato* (Spanish for Flat Nose).

By stealing fresh horses from every ranch they were successful in traversing from seventy-five to one hundred miles a day, killing and destroying all in their path, the culminating point in their bloody career being the butchery of Judge McComas and wife, prominent and refined people of Silver City, N. M., and the abduction of their bright boy, Charlie, whom the Indians carried back with them on their retreat through New Mexico and Chihuahua.

It may serve to give some idea of the courage, boldness, and sublety of these raiders to state that in their dash through Sonora, Arizona, New Mexico, and Chihuahua, a distance of not less than eight hundred miles, they passed at times through localities fairly well settled and close to an aggregate of at least 5,000 troops—4,500 Mexican and 500 American. They killed twenty-five persons, Mexican and American, and lost but two—one killed near the Total Wreck mine, Arizona, and one who fell into the hands of the American troops, of which last much has to be narrated.

To attempt to catch such a band of Apaches by *direct* pursuit would be about as hopeless a piece of business as that of catching so many fleas. All that could be done was done; the country was alarmed by telegraph; people at exposed points put upon their guard, while detachments of troops scoured in every direction, hoping, by good luck, to intercept, retard, mayhap destroy, the daring marauders. The trail they had made coming up from Mexico could, however, be followed *back* to the stronghold; and this, in a military sense, would be the most *direct*, as it would be the most practical pursuit.

Crook's plans soon began to outline themselves. He first concentrated at the most eligible position on the Southern Pacific Railroad—Willcox—all the skeletons of companies which were available, for the protection of Arizona.

Forage, ammunition, and subsistence were brought in on every train; the whole organization was carefully inspected, to secure the rejection of every unserviceable soldier, animal, or weapon; telegrams and letters were sent to the officers commanding the troops of Mexico, but no replies were received, the addresses of the respective generals not being accurately known. As their co-operation was desirable, General Crook, as a last resort, went by railroad to Guaymas, Hermosillo, and Chihuahua, there to see personally and confer with the Mexican civil and military authorities. The cordial reception extended him by all classes was the best evidence of the high regard in which he was held by the inhabitants of the two afflicted States of Sonora and Chihuahua, and of their readiness to welcome any force he would lead to effect the destruction or removal of the common enemy. Generals Topete and Carbó—soldiers of distinction—the governors of the two States, and Mayor Zubiran, of Chihuahua, were most earnest in their desire for a removal of savages whose presence was a cloud upon the prosperity of their fellow-citizens. General Crook made no delay in these conferences, but hurried back to Willcox and marched his command thence to the San Bernardino springs, in the south-east corner of the Territory (Arizona).

But serious delays and serious complications were threatened by the intemperate behavior of an organization calling itself the "Tombstone Rangers," which marched in the direction of the San Carlos Agency with the avowed purpose of "cleaning out" all the Indians there congregated. The chiefs and head men of the Apaches had just caused word to be telegraphed to General Crook that they intended sending him another hundred of their picked warriors as an assurance and pledge that they were not in sympathy with the Chiricahuas on the warpath. Upon learning of the approach of the "Rangers" the chiefs prudently deferred the departure of the new levy of scouts until the horizon should clear, and enable them to see what was to be expected from their white neighbors.

The whiskey taken along by the "Rangers" was exhausted in less than ten days, when the organization expired of thirst, to the gratification of the respectable inhabitants of the frontier, who repudiated an interference with the plans of the military commander, respected and esteemed by them for former distinguished services.

At this point it may be well to insert an outline of the story told by the Chiricahua captive who had been brought down from the San Carlos Agency to Willcox. He said that his name was Pa-nayo-tishn (the Cayote saw him); that he was not a Chiricahua, but a White Mountain Apache of the Dest-chin (or Red Clay) clan, married to two Chiricahua women, by whom he had had children, and with whose people he had lived for years. He had left the Chiricahua stronghold in the mountain called Pa-gotzin-kay some five days' journey below Casas Grandes in Chihuahua. From that stronghold the Chiricahuas had been raiding with impunity upon the Mexicans. When pursued they would draw the Mexicans into the depths of the mountains, ambuscade them, and kill them by rolling down rocks from the heights.

The Chiricahuas had plenty of horses and cattle, but little food of a vegetable character. They were finely provided with sixteen-shooting breech-loading rifles, but were getting short of ammunition, and had made their recent raid into Arizona, hoping to replenish their supply of cartridges. Dissensions had broken out among the chiefs, some of whom, he thought, would be glad to return to the reservation. In making raids they counted upon riding from sixty to seventy-five miles a day as they stole fresh

horses all the time and killed those abandoned.
It would be useless to pursue them, but he
would lead General Crook back along the trail
they had made coming up from Mexico, and he
had no doubt the Chiricahuas could be taken
by surprise.

He had not gone with them of his own free
will, but had been compelled to leave the reservation, and had been badly treated while
with them. The Chiricahuas left the San Carlos because the agent had stolen their rations,
beaten their women, and killed an old squaw.
He asserted emphatically that no communication of any kind had been held with the
Apaches at San Carlos, every attempt in that
direction having been frustrated.

The Chiricahuas, according to Pa-nayo-tishn,
numbered seventy full-grown warriors and fifty
big boys able to fight, with an unknown number
of women and children. In their fights with the
Mexicans about one hundred and fifty had been
killed and captured, principally women and children. The stronghold in the Sierra Madre was
described as a dangerous, rocky, almost inaccessible place, having plenty of wood, water, and

APACHE WAR-DANCE.

grass, but no food except what was stolen from the Mexicans. Consequently the Chiricahuas might be starved out.

General Crook ordered the irons to be struck from the prisoner; to which he demurred, saying he would prefer to wear shackles for the present, until his conduct should prove his sincerity. A half dozen prominent scouts promised to guard him and watch him; so the fetters were removed, and Pa-nayo-tishn or "Peaches," as the soldiers called him, was installed in the responsible office of guide of the contemplated expedition.

By the 22d of April many of the preliminary arrangements had been completed and some of the difficulties anticipated had been smoothed over. Nearly 100 Apache scouts joined the command from the San Carlos Reservation, and in the first hours of night began a war-dance, which continued without a break until the first flush of dawn the next day. They were all in high feather, and entered into the spirit of the occasion with full zest. Not much time need be wasted upon a description of their dresses; they didn't wear any, except breech-clout and moccasins. To the music of an improvised drum and the accompaniment of marrow-freezing yells and shrieks they pirouetted and charged in all directions, swaying their bodies violently, dropping on one knee, then suddenly springing high in air, discharging their pieces, and all the time chanting a rude refrain, in which their own prowess was exalted and that of their enemies alluded to with contempt. Their enthusiasm was not abated by the announcement, quietly diffused, that the "medicine men" had been hard at work, and had succeeded in making a "medicine" which would surely bring the Chiricahuas to grief.

In accordance with the agreement entered into with the Mexican authorities, the American troops were to reach the boundary line *not sooner than May* 1, the object being to let the restless Chiricahuas quiet down as much as possible, and relax their vigilance, while at the same time it enabled the Mexican troops to get into position for effective co-operation.

The convention between our government and that of Mexico, by which a reciprocal crossing of the International Boundary was conceded to the troops of the two republics, stipulated that such crossing should be authorized when the troops were " in close pursuit of a band of savage Indians," and the crossing was made " in the unpopulated or desert parts of said boundary line," which unpopulated or desert parts " had to be two leagues from any encampment or town of either country." The commander of the troops crossing was to give notice at time of crossing, or before if possible, to the nearest military commander or civil authority of the country entered. The pursuing force was to retire to its own territory as soon as it should have fought the band of which it was in pursuit, or lost the trail ; and in no case could it " establish itself or remain in the foreign territory for a longer time than necessary to make the pursuit of the band whose trail it had followed."

The weak points of this convention were the imperative stipulation that the troops should return at once after a fight and the ambiguity of the terms " close pursuit," and " unpopulated country." A friendly expedition from the United States might follow close on the heels

of a party of depredating Apaches, but, under
a rigid construction of the term " unpopulated,"
have to turn back when it had reached some
miserable hamlet exposed to the full ferocity
of savage attack, and most in need of assistance,
as afterwards proved to be the case.

The complication was not diminished by the
orders dispatched by General Sherman on March
31 to General Crook to continue the pursuit of
the Chiricahuas " without regard to departmen-
tal or national boundaries." Both General Crook
and General Topete, anxious to have every difficulty removed which lay in the way of a
thorough adjustment of this vexed question,
telegraphed to their respective governments
asking that a more elastic interpretation be given
to the terms of the convention.

To this telegram General Crook received reply that he must abide strictly by the terms of
the convention, which could only be changed
with the concurrence of the Mexican Senate.
But what these terms meant exactly was left
just as much in the dark as before. On the 23d
of April General Crook moved out from Willcox, accompanied by the Indian scouts and a

force of seven skeleton companies of the Third and Sixth Cavalry, under Colonel James Biddle, guarding a train of wagons, with supplies of ammunition and food for two months. This force, under Colonel Biddle, was to remain in reserve at or near San Bernardino Springs on the Mexican boundary, while its right and left flanks respectively were to be covered by detachments commanded by Rafferty, Vroom, Overton, and Anderson; this disposition affording the best possible protection to the settlements in case any of the Chiricahuas should make their way to the rear of the detachment penetrating Mexico.

A disagreeable sand-storm enveloped the column as it left the line of the Southern Pacific Railroad, preceded by the detachment of Apache scouts. A few words in regard to the peculiar methods of the Apaches in marching and conducting themselves while on a campaign may not be out of place. To veterans of the campaigns of the Civil War familiar with the compact formations of the cavalry and infantry of the Army of the Potomac, the loose, straggling methods of the Apache scouts would appear startling, and yet no soldier would fail to appre-

hend at a glance that the Apache was the perfect, the ideal, scout of the whole world. When
Lieutenant Gatewood, the officer in command,
gave the short, jerky order, Ugashé—Go!—the
Apaches started as if shot from a gun, and in a
minute or less had covered a space of one hundred yards front, which distance rapidly widened as they advanced, at a rough, shambling
walk, in the direction of Dos Cabezas (Two
Heads), the mining camp near which the first
halt was to be made.

They moved with no semblance of regulari-
ty; individual fancy alone governed.   Here
was a clump of three; not far off two more,
and scattered in every point of the compass,
singly or in clusters, were these indefatigable
scouts, with vision as keen as a hawk's, tread
as untiring and as stealthy as the panther's,
and ears so sensitive that nothing escapes them.
An artist, possibly, would object to many of
them as undersized, but in all other respects
they would satisfy every requirement of ana-
tomical criticism.   Their chests were broad,
deep, and full; shoulders perfectly straight;
limbs well-proportioned, strong, and muscular,

APACHE INDIAN SCOUTS EXAMINING TRAILS BY NIGHT.

without a suggestion of undue heaviness; hands
and feet small and taper but wiry; heads
well-shaped, and countenances often lit up with
a pleasant, good-natured expression, which
would be more constant, perhaps, were it not
for the savage, untamed cast imparted by the
loose, disheveled, gypsy locks of raven black,
held away from the face by a broad, flat band
of scarlet cloth. Their eyes were bright, clear,
and bold, frequently expressive of the greatest
good humor and satisfaction. Uniforms had
been issued, but were donned upon ceremonial
occasions only. On the present march each
wore a loosely fitting shirt of red, white, or
gray stuff, generally of calico, in some gaudy
figure, but not infreqently the sombre article of
woollen raiment issued to white soldiers. This
came down outside a pair of loose cotton draw-
ers, reaching to the moccasins. The moccasins
are the most important articles of Apache ap-
parel. In a fight or on a long march they will
discard all else, but under any and every cir-
cumstance will retain the moccasins. These
had been freshly made before leaving Willcox.
The Indian to be fitted stands erect upon the

ground while a companion traces with a sharp knife the outlines of the sole of his foot upon a piece of rawhide. The leggin is made of soft buckskin, attached to the foot and reaching to mid-thigh. For convenience in marching, it is allowed to hang in folds below the knee. The raw-hide sole is prolonged beyond the great toe, and turned upward in a shield, which protects from cactus and sharp stones. A leather belt encircling the waist holds forty rounds of metallic cartridges, and also keeps in place the regulation blue blouse and pantaloons, which are worn upon the person only when the Indian scout is anxious to "paralyze" the frontier towns or millitary posts by a display of all his finery.

The other trappings of these savage auxiliaries are a Springfield breech-loading rifle, army pattern, a canteen full of water, a butcher knife, an awl in leather case, a pair of tweezers, and a tag. The awl is used for sewing moccasins or work of that kind. With the tweezers the Apache young man carefully picks out each and every hair appearing upon his face. The tag marks his place in the tribe, and is in reality nothing more or less than a revival of a plan adopted during the war of the rebellion for the identification of soldiers belonging to the different corps and divisions. Each male Indian at the San Carlos is tagged and numbered, and a descriptive list, corresponding to the tag kept, with a full recital of all his physical peculiarities.

This is the equipment of each and every scout; but there are many, especially the more pious and influential, who carry besides, strapped at the waist, little buckskin bags of Hoddentin, or sacred meal, with which to offer morning and evening sacrifice to the sun or other deity. Others, again, are provided with amulets of lightning-riven twigs, pieces of quartz crystal, petrified wood, concretionary sandstone, galena, or chalchihuitls, or fetiches representing some of their countless planetary gods or Kân, which are regarded as the " dead medicine " for frustrating the designs of the enemy or warding off arrows and bullets in the heat of action. And a few are happy in the possession of priceless sashes and shirts of buckskin, upon which are emblazoned the signs of the sun, moon, lightning, rainbow, hail, fire, the water-beetle, butterfly, snake, centipede, and other powers to which they may appeal for aid in the hour of distress.

The Apache is an eminently religious person, and the more deviltry he plans the more pronounced does his piety become.

The rate of speed attained by the Apaches in marching is about an even four miles an hour on foot, or not quite fast enough to make a horse trot. They keep this up for about fifteen miles, at the end of which distance, if water be encountered and no enemy be sighted, they congregate in bands of from ten to fifteen each, hide in some convenient ravine, sit down, smoke cigarettes, chat and joke, and stretch out in the sunlight, basking like the negroes of the South. If they want to make a little fire, they kindle one with matches, if they happen to have any with them; if not, a rapid twirl, between the palms, of a hard round stick fitting into a circular hole in another stick of softer fiber, will bring fire in from eight to forty-five seconds. The scouts by this time

APACHE AWL CASES, TOBACCO BAGS, AND HEAD DRESSES
WORN BY YOUNG GIRLS.

have painted their faces, daubing them with red ochre, deer's blood, or the juice of roasted "mescal." The object of this is protection from wind and sun, as well as distinctive ornamentation.

The first morning's rest of the Apaches was broken by the shrill cry of Choddi! Choddi! (Antelope! Antelope!) and far away on the left the dull slump! slump! of rifles told that the Apaches on that flank were getting fresh meat for the evening meal. Twenty carcasses demonstrated that they were not the worst of shots; neither were they, by any means, bad cooks.

When the command reached camp these restless, untiring nomads built in a trice all kinds of rude shelters. Those that had the army "dog tents" put them up on frame-works of willow or cotton-wood saplings; others, less fortunate, improvised domiciles of branches covered with grass, or of stones and boards covered with gunny sacks. Before these were finished smoke curled gracefully toward the sky from crackling embers, in front of which, transfixed on wooden spits, were the heads, hearts, and livers of several of the victims of the afternoon's chase. Another addition to the *spolia opima* was a cotton-tailed rabbit, run down by these fleet-footed Bedouins of the South-west. Turkeys and quail are caught in the same manner.

Meanwhile a couple of scouts were making bread,—the light, thin "tortillas" of the Mexicans, baked quickly in a pan, and not bad eating. Two others were fraternally occupied in preparing their bed for the night. Grass was pulled by handfuls, laid upon the ground, and covered with one blanket, another serving as cover. These Indians, with scarcely an exception, sleep with their feet pointed toward little fires, which, they claim, are warm, while the big ones built by the American soldiers, are so hot that they drive people away from them, and, besides, attract the attention of a lurking enemy. At the foot of this bed an Apache was playing on a home-made fiddle, fabricated from the stalk of the "mescal," or American aloe. This fiddle has four strings, and emits a sound like the wail of a cat with its tail caught in a fence. But the noble red

man likes the music, which perhaps is, after
all, not so very much inferior to that of
Wagner.

Enchanted and stimulated by the concord of
sweet sounds, a party of six was playing fiercely
at the Mexican game of "monte," the cards employed being of native manufacture, of horse-
hide, covered with barbarous figures, and well
worthy of a place in any museum.

The cooking was by this time ended, and the
savages, with genuine hospitality, invited the
Americans near them to join in the feast.   It
was not conducive to appetite to glance at dirty
paws tearing bread and meat into fragments ;
yet the meat thus cooked was tender and juicy,
the bread not bad, and the coffee strong and
fairly well made.   The Apaches squatted nearest to the American guests felt it incumbent
upon them to explain everything as the meal
progressed.   They said this (pointing to the
coffee) is Tu-dishishn (black water), and that
Zigosti (bread).

All this time scouts had been posted commanding every possible line of approach.   The
Apache dreads surprise.   It is his own favorite

mode of destroying an enemy, and knowing
what he himself can do, he ascribes to his foe—
no matter how insignificant may be his numbers—the same daring, recklessness, agility,
and subtlety possessed by himself. These Indian scouts will march thirty-five or forty miles
in a day on foot, crossing wide stretches of
waterless plains upon which a tropical sun
beats down with fierceness, or climbing up the
faces of precipitous mountains which stretch
across this region in every direction.

The two great points of superiority of the
native or savage soldier over the representative
of civilized discipline are his absolute knowledge of the country and his perfect ability to
take care of himself at all times and under all
circumstances. Though the rays of the sun
pour down from the zenith, or the scorching
sirocco blow from the south, the Apache scout
trudges along as unconcerned as he was when
the cold rain or snow of winter chilled his
white comrade to the marrow. He finds food,
and pretty good food too, where the Caucasian
would starve. Knowing the habits of wild
animals from his earliest youth, he can catch

turkeys, quail, rabbits, doves, or field-mice, and, perhaps, a prairie-dog or two, which will supply him with meat. For some reason he cannot be induced to touch fish, and bacon or any other product of the hog is eaten only under duress; but the flesh of a horse, mule, or jackass, which has dropped exhausted on the march and been left to die on the trail, is a delicious morsel which the Apache epicure seizes upon wherever possible. The stunted oak, growing on the mountain flanks, furnishes acorns; the Spanish bayonet, a fruit that, when roasted in the ashes of a camp-fire, looks and tastes something like the banana. The whole region of Southern Arizona and Northern Mexico is matted with varieties of the cactus, nearly every one of which is called upon for its tribute of fruit or seed. The broad leaves and stalks of the century-plant—called mescal—are roasted between hot stones, and the product is rich in saccharine matter and extremely pleasant to the taste. The wild potato and the bulb of the "tule" are found in the damp mountain meadows; and the nest of the ground-bee is raided remorselessly for its little store of honey. Sunflower-seeds, when ground fine, are rich and nutritious. Walnuts grow in the deep ravines, and strawberries in favorable locations; in the proper season these, with the seeds of wild grasses and wild pumpkins, the gum of the "mesquite," or the sweet, soft inner bark of the pine, play their part in staving off the pangs of hunger.

The above are merely a few of the resources of the Apache scout when separated from the main command. When his moccasins give out on a long march over the sharp rocks of the mountains or the cutting sands of the plains, a few hours' rest sees him equipped with a new pair,—his own handiwork,—and so with other portions of his raiment. He is never without awl, needle, thread, or sinew. Brought up from infancy to the knowledge and use of arms of some kind,—at first the bow and arrow, and later on the rifle,—he is perfectly at home with his weapons, and knowing from past experience how important they are for his preservation, takes much better care of them than does the white soldier out of garrison.

He does not read the newspapers, but the

great book of nature is open to his perusal, and has been drained of much knowledge which his pale-faced brother would be glad to acquire. Every track in the trail, mark in the grass, scratch on the bark of a tree, explains itself to the "untutored" Apache. He can tell to an hour, almost, when the man or animal making them passed by, and, like a hound, will keep on the scent until he catches up with the object of his pursuit.

In the presence of strangers the Apache soldier is sedate and taciturn. Seated around his little apology for a camp-fire, in the communion of his fellows, he becomes vivacious and conversational. He is obedient to authority, but will not brook the restraints which, under our notions of discipline, change men into machines. He makes an excellent sentinel, and not a single instance can be adduced of property having been stolen from or by an Apache on guard.

He has the peculiarity, noticed among so many savage tribes in various parts of the world, of not caring to give his true name to a stranger; if asked for it, he will either give a wrong one or remain mute and let a comrade answer for

3

him. This rule does not apply where he has
been dubbed with a sobriquet by the white soldiers. In such case he will respond promptly,
and tell the inquirer that he is " Stumpy," " Tom
Thumb," " Bill," " Humpy Sam," or " One-Eyed
Reilly," as the case may be. But there is no
such exception in regard to the dead. Their
names are never mentioned, even by the wailing
friends who loudly chant their virtues.

Approaching the enemy his vigilance is a
curious thing to witness. He avoids appearing
suddenly upon the crest of a hill, knowing that
his figure projected against the sky can at such
time be discerned from a great distance. He will
carefully bind around his brow a sheaf of grass,
or some other foliage, and thus disguised crawl
like a snake to the summit and carefully peer
about, taking in with his keen black eyes the
details of the country to the front with a rapidity and thoroughness the American or Euro-
pean can never acquire. In battle he is again
the antithesis of the Caucasian. The Apache
has no false ideas about courage ; he would prefer to skulk like the cayote for hours, and then
kill his enemy, or capture his herd, rather than,

APACHE AMBUSCADE.

by injudicious exposure, receive a wound, fatal
or otherwise. But he is no coward; on the
contrary, he is entitled to rank among the
bravest. The precautions taken for his safety
prove that he is an exceptionally skillful soldier.
His first duty under fire is to jump for a rock,
bush, or hole, from which no enemy can drive
him except with loss of life or blood.

The policy of Great Britain has always been
to enlist a force of auxiliaries from among the
natives of the countries falling under her sway.
The Government of the United States, on the
contrary, has persistently ignored the really excellent material, ready at hand, which could,
with scarcely an effort and at no expense, be
mobilized, and made to serve as a frontier police.
General Crook is the only officer of our army
who has fully recognized the incalculable value
of a native contingent, and in all his campaigns
of the past thirty-five years has drawn about
him as soon as possible a force of Indians, which
has been serviceable as guides and trailers, and
also of consequence in reducing the strength of
the opposition.

The white army of the United States is a

much better body of officers and men than a critical and censorious public gives it credit for being. It represents intelligence of a high order, and a spirit of devotion to duty worthy of unbounded praise; but it does not represent the acuteness of the savage races. It cannot follow the trail like a dog on the scent. It may be brave and well-disciplined, but its members cannot tramp or ride, as the case may be, from forty to seventy-five miles in a day, without water, under a burning sun. No civilized army can do that. It is one of the defects of civilized training that man develops new wants, awakens new necessities,—becomes, in a word, more and more a creature of luxury.

Take the Apache Indian under the glaring sun of Mexico. He quietly peels off all his clothing and enjoys the fervor of the day more than otherwise. He may not be a great military genius, but he is inured to all sorts of fatigue, and will be hilarious and jovial when the civilized man is about to die of thirst.

Prominent among these scouts was of course first of all " Peaches," the captive guide. He was one of the handsomest men, physically, to

be found in the world. He never knew what
it was to be tired, cross, or out of humor. His
knowledge of the topography of Northern Sonora was remarkable, and his absolute veracity
and fidelity in all his dealings a notable feature
in his character. With him might be mentioned
"Alchise," "Mickey Free," "Severiano," "Nockié-
cholli," "Nott," and dozens of others, all tried
and true men, experienced in warfare and de-
voted to the general whose standard they followed.

II.

From Willcox to San Bernardino Springs, by the road the wagons followed, is an even 100 miles. The march thither, through a most excellent grazing country, was made in five days, by which time the command was joined by Captain Emmet Crawford, Third Cavalry, with more than 100 additional Apache scouts and several trains of pack-mules.

San Bernardino Springs break out from the ground upon the Boundary Line and flow south into the Yaqui River, of which the San Bernardino River is the extreme head. These springs yielded an abundance of water for all our needs, and at one time had refreshed thousands of head of cattle, which have since disappeared under the attrition of constant warfare with the Apaches.

The few days spent at San Bernardino were days of constant toil and labor; from the first streak of dawn until far into the night the task of organizing and arranging went on. Telegrams were dispatched to the Mexican generals notifying them that the American troops would leave promptly by the date agreed upon, and at last the Indian scouts began their war-dances, and continued them without respite from each sunset until the next sunrise. In a conference with General Crook they informed him of their anxiety to put an end to the war and bring peace to Arizona, so that the white men and Apaches could live and work side by side.

By the 29th of April all preparations were complete. Baggage had been cut down to a minimum. Every officer and man was allowed to carry the clothes on his back, one blanket and forty rounds of ammunition. Officers were ordered to mess with the packers and on the same food issued to soldiers and Indian scouts. One hundred and sixty rounds of extra ammunition and rations of hard-bread, coffee and bacon, for sixty days, were carried on pack-mules.

At this moment General Sherman tele-graphed to General Crook that he must not cross the Mexican boundary in pursuit of Indians, except in strict accord with the terms of the treaty, without defining exactly what those terms meant. Crook replied, acknowledging receipt of these instructions and saying that he would respect treaty stipulations.

On Tuesday, May 1st, 1883, the expedition crossed the boundary into Mexico. Its exact composition was as follows: General George Crook, in command. Captain John G. Bourke, Third Cavalry, acting adjutant-general; Lieutenant G. S. Febiger, engineer officer, aid-de-camp; Captain Chaffee, Sixth Cavalry, with Lieutenants West and Forsyth, and forty-two enlisted men of "I" company of that regiment; Doctor Andrews, Private A. F. Harmer of the General Service, and 193 Indian scouts, under Captain Emmet Crawford, Third Cavalry, Lieutenant Mackey, Third Cavalry, and Gatewood, Sixth Cavalry, with whom were Al. Zeiber, McIntosh, "Mickey Free," Severiano, and Sam Bowman, as interpreters.

The pack-mules, for purposes of efficient management, were divided into five trains, each with its complement of skilled packers. These trains were under charge of Monach, Hopkins, Stanfield, " Long Jim Cook," and " Short Jim Cook."

Each packer was armed with carbine and revolver, for self-protection, but nothing could be expected of them, in the event of an attack, beyond looking out for the animals. Consequently the effective fighting strength of the command was a little over fifty white men— officers and soldiers—and not quite 200 Apache scouts, representing the various bands, Chiricahua, White Mountain, Yuma, Mojave, and Tonto.

The first rays of the sun were beaming upon the Eastern hills as we swung into our saddles, and, amid a chorus of good-byes and God-bless-yous from those left behind, pushed down the hot and sandy valley of the San Bernardino, past the mouth of Guadalupe cañon, to near the confluence of Elias Creek, some twenty miles. Here camp was made on the banks of a pellucid stream, under the shadow of graceful walnut and ash trees. The Apache scouts had scoured the country to the front and on both flanks, and returned loaded with deer and wild turkeys, the latter being run down and caught in the bushes. One escaped from its captors and started through camp on a full jump, pursued by the Apaches, who, upon re-catching it, promptly twisted its head off.

The Apaches were in excellent spirits, the " medicine men " having repeated with emphasis the prediction that the expedition was to be a grand success. One of the most influential of them—a mere boy, who carried the most sacred medicine—was especially positive in his views, and, unlike most prophets, backed them up with a bet of $40.

On May 2, 1883, breakfasted at 4 A.M. The train—Monach's—with which we took meals was composed equally of Americans and Mexicans. So, when the cook spread his canvas on the ground, one heard such expressions as *Tantito' zucarito quiero; Sirve pasar el járabe; Pase rebanada de pan; Otra gotita mas de café*, quite as frequently as their English equivalents, " I'd like a little more sugar," "Please pass the sirup," " Hand me a slice of bread," " A little drop of coffee." Close by, the scouts consumed their meals, and with more silence, yet not so silently but that their calls for *inchi* (salt), *ikón* (flour), *pezá-a* (frying-pan), and other articles, could be plainly heard.

Martin, the cook, deserves some notice. He was not, as he himself admitted, a French cook by profession. His early life had been passed in the more romantic occupation of driving an ore-wagon between Willcox and Globe, and, to quote his own proud boast, he could " hold down a sixteen-mule team with any outfit this side the Rio Grande."

But what he lacked in culinary knowledge he more than made up in strength and agility. He was not less than six feet two in his socks, and built like a young Hercules. He was gentle-natured, too, and averse to fighting. Such, at least, was the opinion I gathered from a remark he made the first evening I was thrown into his society.

His eyes somehow were fixed on mine, while he said quietly, "If there's anybody here don't like the grub, I'll kick a lung out of him!" I was just about suggesting that a couple of pounds less saleratus in the bread and a couple of gallons less water in the coffee would be grateful to my Sybarite palate ; but, after this conversation, I reflected that the fewer remarks I made the better would be the chances of my enjoying the rest of the trip; so I said nothing. Martin, I believe, is now in Chihuahua, and I assert from the depths of an outraged stomach, that a better man or a worse cook never thumped a mule or turned a flapjack.

The march was continued down the San Bernardino until we reached its important affluent, the Bávispe, up which we made our way until the first signs of habitancy were encountered in the squalid villages of Bávispe, Basaraca, and Huachinera.

The whole country was a desert. On each hand were the ruins of depopulated and abandoned hamlets, destroyed by the Apaches. The bottom-lands of the San Bernardino, once smiling with crops of wheat and barley, were now covered with a thickly-matted jungle of semitropical vegetation. The river banks were choked by dense brakes of cane of great size and thickness. The narrow valley was hemmed in by rugged and forbidding mountains, gashed

and slashed with a thousand ravines, to cross
which exhausted both strength and patience.
The foot-hills were covered with *chevaux de
frise* of Spanish bayonet, mescal, and cactus.
The lignum-vitæ flaunted its plumage of crim-
son flowers, much like the fuchsia, but growing
in clusters. The grease-wood, ordinarily so
homely, here assumed a garniture of creamy
blossoms, rivaling the gaudy dahlia-like cups
upon the nopal, and putting to shame the mod-
est tendrils pendent from the branches of the
mesquite.

The sun glared down pitilessly, wearing out
the poor mules, which had as much as they
could do to scramble over the steep hills, composed of a nondescript accumulation of lava,
sandstone, porphyry, and limestone, half-
rounded by the action of water, and so loosely
held together as to slip apart and roll away
the instant the feet of animals or men touched
them.

When they were not slipping over loose
stones or climbing rugged hills, they were breaking their way through jungles of thorny vegetation, which tore their quivering flesh. One

of the mules, falling from the rocks, impaled itself upon a mesquite branch, and had to be killed.

Through all this the Apache scouts trudged without a complaint, and with many a laugh and jest. Each time camp was reached they showed themselves masters of the situation. They would gather the saponaceous roots of the yucca and Spanish bayonet, to make use of them in cleaning their long, black hair, or cut sections of the bamboo-like cane and make pipes for smoking, or four-holed flutes, which emitted a weird, Chinese sort of music, responded to with melodious chatter by countless birds perched in the shady seclusion of ash and cotton-wood.

Those scouts who were not on watch gave themselves up to the luxury of the tá-a-chi, or sweat-bath. To construct these baths, a dozen willow or cotton-wood branches are stuck in the ground and the upper extremities, united to form a dome-shaped framework, upon which are laid blankets to prevent the escape of heat. Three or four large rocks are heated and placed in the centre, the Indians arranging themselves around these rocks and bending over them. Silicious bowlders are invariably selected, and not calcareous—the Apaches being sufficiently familiar with rudimentary mineralogy to know that the latter will frequently crack and explode under intense heat.

When it came to my time to enter the sweat-lodge I could see nothing but a network of arms and legs, packed like sardines. An extended experience with Broadway omnibuses assured me that there must always be room for one more. The smile of the " medicine-man " —the master of ceremonies—encouraged me to push in first an arm, then a leg, and, finally, my whole body.

Thump! sounded the damp blanket as it fell against the frame-work and shut out all light and air. The conductor of affairs inside threw a handful of water on the hot rocks, and steam, on the instant, filled every crevice of the den. The heat was that of a bake-oven; breathing was well-nigh impossible.

" Sing," said in English the Apache boy, " Keet," whose legs and arms were sinuously intertwined with mine; " sing heap; sleep moocho

to-night; eat plenny dinna to-mollo." The
other bathers said that everybody must sing.
I had to yield. My *repertoire* consists of but
one song—the lovely ditty—" Our captain's
name is Murphy." I gave them this with all
the lung-power I had left, and was heartily en-
cored; but I was too much exhausted to respond, and rushed out, dripping with perspiration, to plunge with my dusky comrades into
the refreshing waters of the Bávispe, which
had worn out for themselves tanks three to
twenty feet deep. The effects of the bath were
all that the Apaches had predicted—a sound,
refreshing sleep and increased appetite.

The farther we got into Mexico the greater
the desolation. The valley of the Bávispe,
like that of the San Bernardino, had once been
thickly populated; now all was wild and gloomy.
Foot-prints indeed were plenty, but they were
the fresh moccasin-tracks of Chiricahuas, who
apparently roamed with immunity over all this
solitude. There were signs, too, of Mexican
"travel;" but in every case these were "*con-
ductas*" of pack-mules, guarded by companies
of soldiers. Rattlesnakes were encountered

with greater frequency both in camp and on the march. When found in camp the Apaches, from superstitious reasons, refrained from killing them, but let the white men do it.

The vegetation remained much the same as that of Southern Arizona, only denser and larger. The cactus began to bear odorous flowers—a species of night-blooming cereus— and parrots of gaudy plumage flitted about camp, to the great joy of the scouts, who, catching two or three, tore the feathers from their bodies and tied them in their inky locks. Queenly humming-birds of sapphire hue darted from bush to bush and tree to tree. Every one felt that we were advancing into more torrid regions. However, by this time faces and hands were finely tanned and blistered, and the fervor of the sun was disregarded. The nights remained cool and refreshing throughout the trip, and, after the daily march or climb, soothed to the calmest rest.

On the 5th of May the column reached the feeble, broken-down towns of Bávispe and Basaraca. The condition of the inhabitants was deplorable. Superstition, illiteracy, and bad government had done their worst, and, even had not the Chiricahuas kept them in mortal terror, it is doubtful whether they would have had energy enough to profit by the natural advantages, mineral and agricultural, of their immediate vicinity. The land appeared to be fertile and was well watered. Horses, cattle, and chickens throve; the cereals yielded an abundant return; and scarlet blossoms blushed in the waxy-green foliage of the pomegranate.

Every man, woman, and child had gathered in the streets or squatted on the flat roofs of the adobe houses to welcome our approach with cordial acclamations. They looked like a grand national convention of scarecrows and rag-pickers, their garments old and dingy, but no man so poor that he didn't own a gorgeous sombrero, with a snake-band of silver, or display a flaming sash of cheap red silk and wool. Those who had them displayed rainbow-hued *serapes* flung over the shoulders; those who had none went in their shirt-sleeves.

The children were bright, dirty, and pretty; the women so closely enveloped in their *rebozos* that only one eye could be seen. They greeted our people with warmth, and offered to go with us to the mountains. With the volubility of parrots they began to describe a most blood-thirsty fight recently had with the Chiricahuas, in which, of course, the Apaches had been completely and ignominiously routed, each Mexican having performed prodigies of valor on a par with those of Ajax. But at the same time they wouldn't go alone into their fields,— only a quarter of a mile off,—which were constantly patroled by a detachment of twenty-five or thirty men of what was grandiloquently styled the National Guard. " Peaches," the guide, smiled quietly, but said nothing, when told of this latest annihilation of the Chiricahuas. General Crook, without a moment's hesitancy, determined to keep on the trail farther into the Sierra Madre.

The food of these wretched Mexicans was mainly *atole*,—a weak flour-gruel resembling the paste used by our paper-hangers. Books they had none, and newspapers had not yet been heard of. Their only recreation was in religious festivals, occurring with commendable frequency. The churches themselves were in

the last stages of dilapidation; the adobe ex-
teriors showed dangerous indications of approaching dissolution, while the tawdry orna-
ments of the inside were foul and black with
age, smoke, dust, and rain.

I asked a small, open-mouthed boy to hold
my horse for a moment until I had examined
one of these edifices, which bore the elaborate
title of the Temple of the Holy Sepulchre and
our Lady of the Trance. This action evoked a
eulogy from one of the bystanders : " This man
can't be an American, he must be a Christian,"
he sagely remarked ; " he speaks Castilian, and
goes to church the first thing."

It goes without saying that they have no
mails in that country. What they call the
post-office of Basaraca is in the store of the
town. The store had no goods for sale, and
the post-office had no stamps. The postmaster
didn't know when the mail would go ; it used
to go every eight days, but now—*quien sabe?*
Yes, he would send our letters the first opportunity. The price ? Oh ! the price ?—did the
caballeros want to know how much ? Well, for
Mexican people, he charged five cents, but

the Americans would have to pay *dos reales*
(twenty-five cents) for each letter.

The only supplies for sale in Basaraca were
fiery mescal, chile, and a few eggs, eagerly
snapped up by the advance-guard. In making
these purchases we had to enter different
houses, which vied with each other in penury
and destitution. There were no chairs, no ta-
bles, none of the comforts which the humblest
laborers in our favored land demand as right
and essential. The inmates in every instance
received us urbanely and kindly. The women,
who were uncovered inside their domiciles, were
greatly superior in good looks and good breed-
ing to their husbands and brothers; but the
latter never neglected to employ all the punc-
tilious expressions of Spanish politeness.

That evening the round-stomached old man,
whom, in ignorance of the correct title, we all
agreed to call the Alcalde, paid a compliment-
ary visit to General Crook, and with polite
flourishes bade him welcome to the soil of Mexico informed him that he had received orders
to render the expedition every assistance in his
power, and offered to accompany it at the head

of every man and boy in the vicinity. General Crook felt compelled to decline the assistance of these valiant auxiliaries, but asked permission to buy four beeves to feed to the Apache scouts, who did not relish bacon or other salt meat.

Bivouac was made that night on the banks of the Bávispe, under the bluff upon which perched the town of Basaraca. Numbers of visitors—men and boys—flocked in to see us, bringing bread and tobacco for barter and sale. In their turn a large body of our people went up to the town and indulged in the unexpected luxury of a ball. This was so entirely original in all its features that a mention of it is admissible.

Bells were ringing a loud peal, announcing that the morrow would be Sunday, when a prolonged thumping of drums signaled that the *Baile* was about to begin.

Wending our way to the corner whence the noise proceeded, we found that a half-dozen of the packers had bought out the whole stock of the *tienda*, which dealt only in *mescal*, paying therefor the princely sum of $12.50.

Invitations had been extended to all the adult inhabitants to take part in the festivities. For some reason all the ladies sent regrets by the messenger; but of men there was no lack, the packers having taken the precaution to send out a patrol to scour the streets, "collar" and "run in" every male biped found outside his own threshold. These captives were first made to drink a tumbler of *mescal* to the health of the two great nations, Mexico and the United States,—and then were formed into quadrille sets, moving in unison with the orchestra of five pieces,—two drums, two squeaky fiddles, and an accordion.

None of the performers understood a note of music. When a new piece was demanded, the tune had to be whistled in the ears of the bass-drummer, who thumped it off on his instrument, followed energetically by his enthusiastic assistants.

This orchestra was augmented in a few moments by the addition of a young boy with a sax-horn. He couldn't play, and the horn had lost its several keys, but he added to the noise and was welcomed with screams of applause.

It was essentially a *stag* party, but a very funny
one. The new player was doing some good
work when a couple of dancers whirled into
him, knocking him clear off his pins and astride
of the bass-drum and drummer.

Confusion reigned only a moment; good
order was soon restored, and the dance would
have been resumed with increased jollity had
not the head of the bass-drum been helplessly
battered.

Midnight had long since been passed, and
there was nothing to be done but break up the
party and return to camp.

From Basaraca to Tesorababi—over twenty
miles—the line of march followed a country
almost exactly like that before described. The
little hamlets of Estancia and Huachinera were
perhaps a trifle more squalid than Bávispe or
Basaraca, and their churches more dilapidated;
but in that of Huachinera were two or three
unusually good oil-paintings, brought from
Spain a long time ago. Age, dust, weather,
and candle-grease had almost ruined, but had
not fully obliterated, the touch of the master-
hand which had made them.

Tesorababi must have been, a couple of generations since, a very noble ranch. It has plenty of water, great groves of oak and mesquite, with sycamore and cottonwood growing near the water, and very nutritious grass upon the neighboring hills. The buildings have fallen into ruin, nothing being now visible but the stout walls of stone and adobe. Mesquite trees of noble size choke up the corral, and everything proclaims with mute eloquence the supremacy of the Apache.

Alongside of this ranch are the ruins of an ancient pueblo, with quantities of broken pottery, stone mortars, Obsidian flakes and kindred *reliquiæ.*

To Tesorababi the column was accompanied by a small party of guides sent out by the Alcalde of Basaraca. General Crook ordered them back, as they were not of the slightest use so long as we had such a force of Apache scouts.

We kept in camp at Tesorababi until the night of May 7, and then marched straight for the Sierra Madre. The foot-hills were thickly covered with rich *grama* and darkened by groves of scrub-oak. Soon the oak gave way to cedar in great abundance, and the hills and ridges became steeper as we struck the trail lately made by the Chiricahuas driving off cattle from Sahuaripa and Oposura. We were fairly within the range, and had made good progress, when the scouts halted and began to explain to General Crook that nothing but bad luck could be expected if he didn't set free an owl which one of our party had caught, and tied to the pommel of his saddle.

They said the owl (Bû) was a bird of ill-omen, and that we could not hope to whip the Chiricahuas so long as we retained it. These solicitations bore good fruit. The moon-eyed bird of night was set free and the advance resumed. Shortly before midnight camp was made in a very deep cañon, thickly wooded, and having a small stream a thousand feet below our position. No fires were allowed, and some confusion prevailed among the pack-mules, which could not find their places.

Very early the next morning (May 8, 1883) the command moved in easterly direction up the cañon. This was extremely rocky and steep. Water stood in pools everywhere, and animals

and men slaked their fierce thirst. Indications
of Chiricahua depredations multiplied. The trail
was fresh and well-beaten, as if by scores—yes,
hundreds—of stolen ponies and cattle.

The carcasses of five freshly slaughtered
beeves lay in one spot; close to them a couple
more, and so on.

The path wound up the face of the mountain,
and became so precipitous that were a horse to
slip his footing he would roll and fall hundreds
of feet to the bottom. At one of the abrupt
turns could be seen, deep down in the cañon,
the mangled fragments of a steer which had
fallen from the trail, and been dashed to pieces
on the rocks below. It will save much repetition to say, at this point, that from now on we
were never out of sight of ponies and cattle,
butchered, in every stage of mutilation, or alive,
and roaming by twos and threes in the ravines
and on the mountain flanks.

Climb! Climb! Climb! Gaining the sum-
mit of one ridge only to learn that above it tow-
ered another, the face of nature fearfully cor-
rugated into a perplexing alternation of ridges
and chasms. Not far out from the last bivouac

was passed the spot where a large body of Mexican troops had camped, the farthest point of their penetration into the range, although their scouts had been pushed in some distance farther, only to be badly whipped by the Chiricahuas, who sent them flying back, utterly demoralized·

These particulars may now be remarked of that country: It seemed to consist of a series of parallel and very high, knife-edged hills,—extremely rocky and bold ; the cañons all contained water, either flowing rapidly, or else in tanks of great depth. Dense pine forests covered the ridges near the crests, the lower skirts being matted with scrub-oak. Grass was generally plentiful, but not invariably to be depended upon. Trails ran in every direction, and upon them were picked up all sorts of odds and ends plundered from the Mexicans,—dresses, made and unmade, saddles, bridles, letters, flour, onions, and other stuff. In every sheltered spot could be discerned the ruins,—buildings, walls, and dams, erected by an extinct race, once possessing this region.

The pack-trains had much difficulty in getting along. Six mules slipped from the trail, and rolled over and over until they struck the bottom of the cañon. Fortunately they had selected a comparatively easy grade, and none was badly hurt.

The scouts became more and more vigilant and the " medicine-men " more and more devotional. When camp was made the high peaks were immediately picketed, and all the approaches carefully examined. Fires were allowed only in rare cases, and in positions affording absolute concealment. Before going to bed the scouts were careful to fortify themselves in such a manner that surprise was simply impossible.

Late at night (May 8th) the " medicine-men " gathered together for the never-to-be-neglected duty of singing and " seeing " the Chiricahuas. After some palaver I succeeded in obtaining the privilege of sitting in the circle with them. All but one chanted in a low, melancholy tone, half song and half grunt. The solitary exception lay as if in a trance for a few moments, and then, half opening his lips, began to thump himself violently in the breast, and to point to the east and north, while he muttered : " Me

can't see the Chilicahuas yet. Bimeby me see
'um. Me catch 'um, me kill 'um. Me no catch
'um, me no kill 'um. Mebbe so six day me
catch 'um ; mebbe so two day. Tomollow me
send twenty-pibe (25) men to hunt 'um tlail.
Mebbe so tomollow catch 'um squaw. Chilicahua see me, me no get 'um. No see me,
me catch him. Me see him little bit now.
Mebbe so me see 'um more tomollow. Me
catch 'um, me kill 'um. Me catch 'um hoss, me
catch 'um mool (mule), me catch 'um cow. Me
catch Chilicahua pooty soon, bimeby. Me kill
'um heap, and catch 'um squaw." These prophe-
cies, translated for me by an old friend in the
circle who spoke some English, were listened to
with rapt attention and reverence by the awe-
struck scouts on the exterior.

The succeeding day brought increased trouble
and danger. The mountains became, if anything, steeper; the trails, if anything, more
perilous. Carcasses of mules, ponies, and cows
lined the path along which we toiled, dragging
after us worn-out horses.

It was not yet noon when the final ridge of
the day was crossed and the trail turned down

a narrow, gloomy, and rocky gorge, which gradually widened into a small amphitheatre.

This, the guide said, was the stronghold occupied by the Chiricahuas while he was with
them; but no one was there now. For all purposes of defense, it was admirably situated.
Water flowed in a cool, sparkling stream
through the middle of the amphitheatre. Pine,
oak, and cedar in abundance and of good size
clung to the steep flanks of the ridges, in whose
crevices grew much grass. The country, for a
considerable distance, could be watched from
the pinnacles upon which the savage pickets
had been posted, while their huts had been so
scattered and concealed in the different brakes
that the capture or destruction of the entire
band could never have been effected.

The Chiricahuas had evidently lived in this
place a considerable time. The heads and bones
of cows and ponies were scattered about on all
sides. Meat must have been their principal
food, since we discovered scarcely any mescal
or other vegetables. At one point the scouts
indicated where a mother had been cutting a
child's hair; at another, where a band of young-

sters had been enjoying themselves sliding down rocks.

Here were picked up the implements used by a young Chiricahua assuming the duties of manhood. Like all other Indians they make vows and pilgrimages to secluded spots, during which periods they will not put their lips to water, but suck up all they need through a quill or cane. Hair-brushes of grass, bows and arrows, and a Winchester rifle had likewise been left behind by the late occupants.

The pack-trains experienced much difficulty in keeping the trail this morning (May 9). Five mules fell over the precipice and killed themselves, three breaking their necks and two having to be shot.

Being now in the very centre of the hostile country, May 10, 1883, unusual precautions were taken to guard against discovery or ambuscade, and to hurry along the pack-mules. Parties of Apache scouts were thrown out to the front, flanks, and rear to note carefully every track in the ground. A few were detailed to stay with the pack-mules and guide them over the best line of country. Ax-men

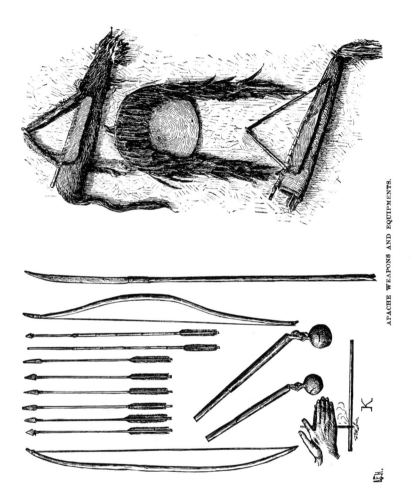

APACHE WEAPONS AND EQUIPMENTS.

were sent ahead on the trail to chop out trees and remove rocks or other obstructions. Then began a climb which reflected the experience of the previous two days ; if at all different, it was much worse. Upon the crest of the first high ridge were seen forty abandoned *jacales* or lodges of branches; after that, another dismantled village of thirty more, and then, in every protected nook, one, two, or three, as might be. Fearful as this trail was the Chiricahuas had forced over it a band of cattle and ponies, whose footprints had been fully outlined in the mud, just hardened into clay.

After two miles of a very hard climb we slid down the almost perpendicular face of a high bluff of slippery clay and loose shale into an open space dotted with Chiricahua huts, where, on a grassy space, the young savages had been playing their favorite game of mushka, or lance-billiards.

Two white-tailed deer ran straight into the long file of scouts streaming down hill; a shower of rocks and stones greeted them, and there was much suppressed merriment, but not the least bit of noisy laughter, the orders being to avoid any cause of alarm to the enemy.

5

A fearful chute led from this point down into the gloomy chasm along which trickled the head-waters of the Bávispe, gathering in basins and pools clear as mirrors of crystal. A tiny cascade babbled over a ledge of limestone and filled at the bottom a dark-green reservoir of unknown depth. There was no longer any excitement about Chiricahua signs; rather, wonder when none were to be seen.

The ashes of extinct fires, the straw of unused beds, the skeleton frame-work of dismantled huts, the play-grounds and dance-grounds, mescal-pits and acorn-meal mills were visible at every turn. The Chiricahuas must have felt perfectly secure amid these towering pinnacles of rock in these profound chasms, by these bottomless pools of water, and in the depths of this forest primeval. Here no human foe could hope to conquer them. Notwithstanding this security of position, "Peaches" asserted that the Chiricahuas never relaxed vigilance. No fires were allowed at night, and all cooking was done at midday. Sentinels lurked in every crag, and bands of bold raiders kept the foot-hills thoroughly explored. Crossing

Bávispe, the trail zigzagged up the vertical slope of a promontory nearly a thousand feet above the level of the water. Perspiration streamed from every brow, and mules and horses panted, sweated, and coughed; but Up! Up! Up! was the watchword.

Look out! came the warning cry from those in the lead, and then those in the rear and bottom dodged nervously from the trajectory of rocks dislodged from the parent mass, and, gathering momentum as each bound hurled them closer to the bottom of the cañon. To look upon the country was a grand sensation; to travel in it, infernal. Away down at the foot of the mountains the pack-mules could be discerned—apparently not much bigger than jack-rabbits,—struggling and panting up the long, tortuous grade. And yet, up and down these ridges the Apache scouts, when the idea seized them, ran like deer.

One of them gave a low cry, half whisper, half whistle. Instantly all were on the alert, and by some indefinable means, the news flashed through the column that two Chirica-huas had been sighted a short distance ahead

in a side cañon. Before I could write this
down the scouts had stripped to the buff,
placed their clothing in the rocks, and dispatched ten or twelve of their number in swift
pursuit.

This proved to be a false alarm, for in an
hour they returned, having caught up with the
supposed Chiricahuas, who were a couple of
our own packers, off the trail, looking for stray
mules.

When camp was made that afternoon the
Apache scouts had a long conference with
General Crook. They called attention to the
fact that the pack-trains could not keep up
with them, that five mules had been killed on
the trail yesterday, and five others had rolled
off this morning, but been rescued with slight
injuries. They proposed that the pack-trains
and white troops remain in camp at this point,
and in future move so as to be a day's march
or less behind the Apache scouts, 150 of whom,
under Crawford, Gatewood, and Mackey, with
Al. Zeiber and the other white guides, would
move out well in advance to examine the
country thoroughly in front.

If they came upon scattered parties of the hostiles they would attack boldly, kill as many as they could, and take the rest back, prisoners, to San Carlos. Should the Chiricahuas be intrenched in a strong position, they would engage them, but do nothing rash, until reinforced by the rest of the command. General Crook told them they must be careful not to kill women or children, and that all who surrendered should be taken back to the reservation and made to work for their own living like white people.

Animation and bustle prevailed everywhere; small fires were burning in secluded nooks, and upon the bright embers the scouts baked quantities of bread to be carried with them. Some ground coffee on flat stones; others examined their weapons critically and cleaned their cartridges. Those whose moccasins needed repair sewed and patched them, while the more cleanly and more religious indulged in the sweat-bath, which has a semi-sacred character on such occasions.

A strong detachment of packers, soldiers, and Apaches climbed the mountains to the south, and reached the locality in the foot-hills where the Mexicans and Chiricahuas had recently had an engagement. Judging by signs it would appear conclusive that the Indians had enticed the Mexicans into an ambuscade, killed a number with bullets and rocks, and put the rest to ignominious flight. The "medicine-men" had another song and pow-wow after dark. Before they adjourned it was announced that in two days, counting from the morrow, the scouts would find the Chiricahuas, and in three days kill a " heap."

On May 11, 1883 (Friday), one hundred and fifty Apache scouts, under the officers above named, with Zeiber, "Mickey Free," Severiano, Archie McIntosh, and Sam Bowman, started from camp, on foot, at daybreak. Each carried on his person four days' rations, a canteen, 100 rounds of ammunition, and a blanket. Those who were to remain in camp picketed the three high peaks overlooking it, and from which half a dozen Chiricahuas could offer serious annoy- ance. Most of those not on guard went down to the water, bathed, and washed clothes. The severe climbing up and down rough mountains, slipping, falling, and rolling in dust and clay, had blackened most of us like negroes.

Chiricahua ponies had been picked up in numbers, four coming down the mountains of their own accord, to join our herds; and altogether, twenty were by this date in camp. The suggestions of the locality were rather peaceful in type; lovely blue humming-birds flitted from bush to bush, and two Apache doll-babies lay upon the ground.

Just as the sun was sinking behind the hills in the west, a runner came back with a note from Crawford, saying there was a fine camping place twelve or fifteen miles across the mountains to the south-east, with plenty of wood, water, and grass.

For the ensuing three days the white soldiers and pack-trains cautiously followed in the footsteps of Crawford and the scouts, keeping a sufficient interval between the two bodies to insure thorough investigation of the rough country in front. The trail did not improve very much, although after the summit of a high, grassy plateau had been gained, there was easy traveling for several leagues. Pine-trees

of majestic proportions covered the mountain-
tops, and there was the usual thickness of
scrub-oak on the lower elevations.   By the side
of the trail, either thrown away or else *cachéd*
in the trees, were quantities of goods left by
the Chiricahuas—calico, clothing, buckskin,
horse-hides, beef-hides, dried meat, and things
of that nature.   The nights were very cool, the
days bright and warm.   The Bávispe and its
tributaries were a succession of deep tanks of
glassy, pure water, in which all our people
bathed on every opportunity.   The scouts
escorting the pack-trains gathered in another
score of stray ponies and mules, and were encouraged by another note sent back by Crawford, saying that he had passed the site of
a Chiricahua village of ninety-eight *wickyups*
(huts), that the enemy had a great drove of
horses and cattle, and that the presence of
Americans or Apache scouts in the country
was yet undreamed of.

Additional rations were pushed ahead to
Crawford and his command, the pack-trains
in rear taking their own time to march.
There was an abundance of wood in the for-

est, grass grew in sufficiency, and the Bávispe
yielded water enough for a great army. The
stream was so clear that it was a pleasure to
count the pebbles at the bottom and to watch
the graceful fishes swimming within the
shadow of moss-grown rocks. The current
was so deep that, sinking slowly, with up-
lifted arms, one was not always able to touch
bottom with the toes, and so wide that twenty
good, nervous strokes barely sufficed to propel
the swimmer from shore to shore. The water
was soft, cool, and refreshing, and a plunge
beneath its ripples smoothed away the wrinkles
of care.

On May 15, 1883, we climbed and marched
ten or twelve miles to the south-east, crossing
a piece of country recently burned over, the
air, filled with soot and hot dust, blackening
and blistering our faces. Many more old ruins
were passed and scores of walls of masonry.
The trail was slightly improved, but still bad
enough ; the soil, a half-disintegrated, reddish
feldspar, with thin seams of quartz crystals.
There were also granite, sandstone, shale, quart-
zite, and round masses of basalt. In the bot-

toms of the cañons were all kinds of "float "—
granite, basalt, sandstone, porphyry, schist,
limestone, etc.; but no matter what the kind
of rock was, when struck upon the hill-sides it
was almost invariably split and broken, and
grievously retarded the advance.

III.

ABOUT noon of the 15th we had descended into a small box cañon, where we were met by two white men (packers) and nine Apache scouts.

They had come back from Crawford with news for which all were prepared. The enemy was close in our front, and fighting might begin at any moment. The scouts in advance had picked up numbers of ponies, mules, burros, and cattle. This conversation was broken by the sudden arrival of an Apache runner, who had come six miles over the mountains in less than an hour. He reached us at 1.05, and handed General Crook a note, dated 12.15, stating that the advance-guard had run across the Chiricahuas this morning in a cañon, and had become much excited. Two Chiricahuas were fired at, two bucks and a squaw, by scouts, which action had alarmed the hostiles, and their camp was on the move. Crawford would pursue with all possible rapidity. At the same moment reports of distant musketry-firing were borne across the hills. Crawford was fighting the Chiricahuas! There could be no doubt about that; but exactly how many he had found, and what luck he was having, no one could tell. General Crook ordered Chaffee to mount his men, and everybody to be in readiness to move forward to Crawford's support, if necessary. The firing continued for a time, and then grew feeble and died away.

All were anxious for a fight which should bring this Chiricahua trouble to an end; we had an abundance of ammunition and a sufficiency of rations for a pursuit of several days and nights, the moon being at its full.

Shortly after dark Crawford and his command came into camp. They had "jumped" "Bonito's" and "Chato's" *rancherías*, killing nine and capturing five—two boys, two girls, and one young woman, the daughter of "Bonito," without loss to our side. From the dead Chiracahuas had been taken four nickel-plated, breech-loading Winchester repeating rifles, and one Colt's revolver, new model. The

Chiricahuas had been pursued across a fearfully broken country, gashed with countless
ravines, and shrouded with a heavy growth of
pine and scrub-oak. How many had been
killed and wounded could never be definitely
known, the meagre official report, submitted by
Captain Crawford, being of necessity confined
to figures known to be exact. Although the
impetuosity of the younger scouts had precipi-
tated the engagement and somewhat impaired
its effect, yet this little skirmish demonstrated
two things to the hostile Chiricahuas; their
old friends and relatives from the San Carlos
had invaded their strongholds as the allies of
the white men, and could be depended upon
to fight, whether backed up by white soldiers
or not. The scouts next destroyed the village, consisting of thirty *wickyups*, disposed in
two clusters, and carried off all the animals,
loading down forty-seven of them with plun-
der. This included the traditional riffraff of
an Indian village : saddles, bridles, meat, mescal, blankets, and clothing, with occasional
prizes of much greater value, originally stolen
by the Chiricahuas in raids upon Mexicans or

Americans. There were several gold and silver watches, a couple of albums, and a considerable sum of money—Mexican and American coin and paper. The captives behaved with great coolness and self-possession, considering their tender years. The eldest said that her people had been astounded and dismayed when they saw the long line of Apache scouts rushing in upon them; they would be still more disconcerted when they learned that our guide was "Peaches," as familiar as themselves with every nook in strongholds so long regarded as inaccessible. Nearly all the Chiricahua warriors were absent raiding in Sonora and Chihuahua. This young squaw was positive that the Chiricahuas would give up without further fighting, since the Americans had secured all the advantages of position. "Loco" and "Chihuahua," she knew, would be glad to live peaceably upon the reservation, if justly treated; "Hieronymo" and "Chato" she wasn't sure about. "Ju" was defiant, but none of his bands were left alive. Most important information of all, she said that in the *rancheria* just destroyed was a little white boy about six

APACHE GIRL WITH TYPICAL DRESS.

years old, called "Charlie," captured by
"Chato" in his recent raid in Arizona. This
boy had run away with the old squaws when
the advance of the Apache scouts had been first
detected. She said that if allowed to go out
she would in less than two days bring in the
whole band, and Charlie (McComas) with them.
All that night the lofty peak, the scene of the
action, blazed with fire from the burning *rancheria*. Rain-clouds gathered in the sky, and,
after hours of threatening, broke into a severe
but brief shower about sunrise next morning
(May 15).

The young woman was given a little hard
bread and meat, enough to last two days, and
allowed to go off, taking with her the elder of
the boy captives. The others stayed with us and
were kindly treated. They were given all the
baked mescal they could eat and a sufficiency
of bread and meat. The eldest busied herself
with basting a skirt, but, like another Penelope,
as fast as her work was done she ripped it up
and began anew—apparently afraid that idleness would entail punishment. The younger
girl sobbed convulsively, but her little brother,

a handsome brat, gazed stolidly at the world through eyes as big as oysters and as black as jet.

Later in the morning, after the fitful showers had turned into a blinding, soaking rain, the Apache scouts made for these young captives a little shelter of branches and a bed of boughs and dry grass. Pickets were thrown out to watch the country on all sides and seize upon any stray Chiricahua coming unsuspectingly within their reach. The rain continued with exasperating persistency all day. The night cleared off bitter cold and water froze in pails and kettles. The command moved out from this place, going to another and better location a few miles south-east. The first lofty ridge had been scaled, when we descried on the summit of a prominent knoll directly in our front a thin curl of smoke wreathing upwards. This was immediately answered by the scouts, who heaped up pine-cones and cedar branches, which, in a second after ignition, shot a bold, black, resinous signal above the tops of the loftiest pines.

Five miles up and down mountains of no great height but of great asperity led to a fine camping-place, at the junction of two well-watered cañons, near which grew pine, oak, and cedar in plenty, and an abundance of rich, juicy grasses. The Apache scouts sent up a second smoke signal, promptly responded to from a neighboring butte. A couple of minutes after two squaws were seen threading their way down through the timber and rocks and yelling with full voice. They were the sisters of Tò-klani (Plenty Water), one of the scouts. They said that they had lost heavily in the fight, and that while endeavoring to escape over the rocks and ravines and through the timber the fire of the scouts had played havoc among them. They fully confirmed all that the captives had said about Charlie McComas. Two hours had scarcely passed when six other women had come in, approaching the pickets two and two, and waving white rags. One of these, the sister of "Chihuahua"—a prominent man among the Chiricahuas—said that her brother wanted to come in, and was trying to gather up his band, which had scattered like sheep after the fight; he might be looked for in our camp at any moment.

6

On the 18th (May, 1883), before 8.30 A. M., six new arrivals were reported—four squaws, one buck and a boy. Close upon their heels followed sixteen others—men, women, and young children. In this band was " Chihuahua " himself, a fine-looking man, whose countenance betokened great decision and courage.

This chief expressed to General Crook his earnest desire for peace, and acknowledged that all the Chiricahuas could hope to do in the future would be to prolong the contest a few weeks and defer their destruction. He was tired of fighting. His village had been destroyed and all his property was in our hands. He wished to surrender his band just as soon as he could gather it together. " Hieronymo," " Chato," and nearly all the warriors were absent, fighting the Mexicans, but he (" Chihuahua ") had sent runners out to gather up his band and tell his people they must surrender, without reference to what the others did.

Before night forty-five Chiricahuas had come in—men, women, and children. " Chihuahua " asked permission to go out with two young men and hurry his people in. This was granted. He promised to return without any delay. The women of the Chiricahuas showed the wear and tear of a rugged mountain life, and the anxieties and disquietudes of a rugged Ishmaelitish war. The children were models of grace and beauty, which revealed themselves through dirt and rags.

On May 19, 1883, camp was moved five or six miles to a position giving the usual abundance of water and rather better grass. It was a small park in the centre of a thick growth of young pines. Upon unsaddling, the Chiricahuas were counted, and found to number seventy, which total before noon had swollen to an even hundred, not including " Chihuahua " and those gone back with him.

The Chiricahuas were reserved, but goodhumored. Several of them spoke Spanish fluently. Rations were issued in small quantity, ponies being killed for meat. Two or three of the Indians bore fresh bullet-wounds from the late fight. On the succeeding evening, May 20, 1883, the Chiricahuas were again numbered at breakfast. They had increased to

121—sixty being women and girls, the remainder, old men, young men, and boys.

All said that "Chihuahua" and his comrades were hard at work gathering the tribe together and sending them in.

Toward eight o'clock a fearful hubbub was heard in the tall cliffs overlooking camp; Indians fully armed could be descried running about from crag to crag, evidently much perplexed and uncertain what to do. They began to interchange cries with those in our midst, and, after a brief interval, a couple of old squaws ventured down the face of the precipice, followed at irregular distances by war riors, who hid themselves in the rocks half-way down.

They asked whether they were to be hurt if they came in.

One of the scouts and one of the Chiricahuas went out to them to say that it made no difference whether they came in or not; that "Chihuahua" and all his people had surrendered, and that if these new arrivals came in during the day they should not be harmed; that until "Chihuahua" and the last of his band had had

a chance to come in and bring Charlie McComas
hostilities should be suspended. The Chiricahuas were still fearful of treachery and hung
like hawks or vultures to the protecting shad-
ows of inaccessible pinnacles one thousand feet
above our position. Gradually their fears wore
off, and in parties of two and three, by various
trails, they made their way to General Crook's
fire. They were a band of thirty-six warriors,
led by "Hieronymo," who had just returned
from a bloody foray in Chihuahua. "Hieronymo" expressed a desire to have a talk; but
General Crook declined to have anything to do
with him or his party beyond saying that they
had now an opportunity to see for themselves
that their own people were against them; that
we had penetrated to places vaunted as impregnable; that the Mexicans were coming in from
all sides; and that "Hieronymo" could make
up his mind for peace or war just as he chose.

This reply disconcerted "Hieronymo;" he
waited for an hour, to resume the conversation,
but received no encouragement. He and his
warriors were certainly as fine-looking a lot of
pirates as ever cut a throat or scuttled a ship;

not one among them who was not able to travel forty to fifty miles a day over these gloomy precipices and along these gloomy cañons. In muscular development, lung and heart power, they were, without exception, the finest body of human beings I had ever looked upon. Each was armed with a breech-loading Winchester; most had nickel-plated revolvers of the latest pattern, and a few had also bows and lances. They soon began to talk with the Apache scouts, who improved the occasion to inform them that not only had they come down with General Crook, but that from both Sonora and Chihuahua Mexican soldiers might be looked for in swarms.

"Hieronymo" was much humbled by this, and went a second time to General Crook to have a talk. He assured him that he had always wanted to be at peace, but that he had been as much sinned against as sinning; that he had been ill-treated at the San Carlos and driven away; that the Mexicans had been most treacherous in their dealings with his people, and that he couldn't believe a word they said. They had made war upon his women and children, but

had run like coyotes from his soldiers. He had
been trying to open communications with the
Mexican generals in Chihuahua to arrange for
an exchange of prisoners. If General Crook
would let him go back to San Carlos, and guar-
antee him just treatment, he would gladly work
for his own living, and follow the path of peace.
He simply asked for a trial; if he could not
make peace, he and his men would die in these
mountains, fighting to the last. He was not a
bit afraid of Mexicans alone; but he could not
hope to prolong a contest with Mexicans and
Americans united, in these ranges, and with so
many Apache allies assisting them. General
Crook said but little; it amounted to this: that
"Hieronymo" could make up his mind as to
what he wanted, peace or war.

May 21st was one of the busiest days of the
expedition. "Hieronymo," at early dawn, came
to see General Crook, and told him he wished for
peace. He earnestly promised amendment, and
begged to be taken back to San Carlos. He
asked permission to get all his people together,
and said he had sent some of his young men off
to hurry them in from all points. He could not

get them to answer his signals, as they imagined them to be made by Apache scouts trying to ensnare them. Chiricahuas were coming in all the morning,—all ages, and both sexes,—sent in by "Chihuahua" and his party; most of these were mounted on good ponies, and all drove pack and loose animals before them. Early in the day there was seen winding through the pine timber a curious procession,—mostly young warriors, of an aggregate of thirty-eight souls,— driving steers and work cattle, and riding ponies and burros. All these were armed with Winchester and Springfield breech-loaders, with revolvers and lances whose blades were old cavalry sabres. The little boys carried revolvers, lances, and bows and arrows. This was the band of Kaw-tenné (Looking-Glass), a young chief, who claimed to be a Mexican Apache and to belong to the Sierra Madre, in whose recesses he had been born and raised.

The question of feeding all these mouths was getting to be a very serious one. We had started out with sixty days' supplies, one-third of which had been consumed by our own command, and a considerable percentage lost or damaged when

APACHE WARFARE.

mules rolled over the precipices. The great
heat of the sun had melted much bacon, and
there was the usual wastage incident to move-
ments in campaign. Stringent orders were given
to limit issues to the lowest possible amount;
while the Chiricahuas were told that they must
cut and roast all the mescal to be found, and
kill such cattle and ponies as could be spared.
The Chiricahua young men assumed the duty
of butchering the meat. Standing within five
or six feet of a steer, a young buck would prod
the doomed beast one lightning lance-thrust
immediately behind the left fore-shoulder, and,
with no noise other than a single bellow of fear
and agony, the beef would fall forward upon its
knees, dead.

Camp at this period presented a medley of
noises not often found united under a military
standard. Horses were neighing, mules braying,
and bells jingling, as the herds were brought
in to be groomed. The ring of axes against the
trunks of stout pines and oaks, the hum of voices,
the squalling of babies, the silvery laughter of
children at play, and the occasional music of an
Apache fiddle or flute, combined in a pleasant

discord which left the listener uncertain whether
he was in the bivouac of grim-visaged war or
among a band of school-children.   Our Apache
scouts—the Tontos especially—treated the Chiricahuas with dignified reserve : the Sierra Blan-
cas (White Mountain) had intermarried with
them, and were naturally more familiar, but all
watched their rifles and cartridges very carefully to guard against treachery.   The squaws
kept at work, jerking and cooking meat and
mescal for consumption on the way back to San
Carlos.   The entrails were the coveted portions,
for the possession of which the more greedy or
more muscular fought with frequency.

Two of these copper-skinned "ladies" engaged
in a pitched battle ; they rushed for each other
like a couple of infuriated Texas steers ; hair
flew, blood dripped from battered noses, and
two " human forms divine " were scratched and
torn by sharp nails accustomed to this mode of
warfare.   The old squaws chattered and gab-
bled, little children screamed and ran, warriors
stood in a ring, and from a respectful distance
gazed stolidly upon the affray.   No one dared
to interfere.   There is no tiger more dangerous

than an infuriated squaw ; she's a fiend incarnate. The packers and soldiers looked on, discussing the "points" of the belligerents. "The little one's built like a hired man," remarks one critic. "Ya-as ; but the old un's a *He*, and doan' you forgit it." Two rounds settled the battle in favor of the older contestant, although the younger remained on the ground, her bleeding nostrils snorting defiance, her eyes blazing fire, and her tongue volleying forth Apache imprecations.

But all interest was withdrawn from this spectacle and converged upon a file of five wretched, broken-down Mexican women, one of whom bore a nursing baby, who had come within the boundaries of our camp and stood in mute terror, wonder, joy, and hope, unable to realize that they were free. They were a party of captives seized by "Hieronymo" in his last raid into Chihuahua. When washed, rested, and fed a small amount of food, they told a long, rambling story, which is here condensed : They were the wives of Mexican soldiers captured near one of the stations of the Mexican Central Railway just two weeks previously. Originally there had been six in the party, but "Hieronymo" had sent back the oldest and feeblest with a letter to the Mexican general, saying that he wanted to make peace with the whites, and would do so, provided the Mexicans returned the Apache women and children held prisoners by them; if they refused, he would steal all the Mexican women and children he could lay hands on, and keep them as hostages, and would continue the war until he had made Sonora and Chihuahua a desert. The women went on to say that the greatest terror prevailed in Chihuahua at the mere mention of the name of "Hieronymo," whom the peasantry believed to be the devil, sent to punish them for their sins.

"Hieronymo" had killed the Mexican soldiers with rocks, telling his warriors he had no ammunition to waste upon Mexicans. The women had suffered incredible torture climbing the rough skirts of lofty ranges, fording deep streams of icy-cold water, and breaking through morasses, jungles and forests. Their garments had been rent into rags by briars and brambles, feet and ankles scratched, torn, and swollen by contusions from sharp rocks. They said that

when "Hieronymo" had returned to the heart
of the mountains, and had come upon one of
our lately abandoned camps, his dismay was
curious to witness. The Chiricahuas with him
made a hurried but searching examination of
the neighborhood, satisfied themselves that their
enemies—the Americans—had gained access to
their strongholds, and that they had with them
a multitude of Apache scouts, and then started
away in the direction of our present bivouac,
paying no further heed to the captured women
or to the hundreds of stolen stock they were
driving away from Chihuahua. It may be well
to anticipate a little, and say that the cattle in
question drifted out on the back trail, getting
into the foot-hills and falling into the hands of
the Mexicans in pursuit, who claimed their
usual wonderful "victory." The women did
not dare to turn back, and, uncertain what
course to pursue, stayed quietly by the half-dead
embers of our old camp-fires, gathering up a
few odds and ends of rags with which to cover
their nakedness; and of castaway food, which
they devoured with the voracity of famished
wolves. When morning dawned they arose,

half frozen, from the couches they had made, and staggered along in the direction taken by the fleeing Chiricahuas, whom, as already narrated, they followed to where they now were.

And now they were free! Great God! Could it be possible?

The gratitude of these poor, ignorant, broken-down creatures welled forth in praise and glorification to God. "Praise be to the All-Powerful God!" ejaculated one. "And to the most Holy Sacrament!" echoed her companions. "Thanks to our Blessed Lady of Guadalupe!" "And to the most Holy Mary, Virgin of Soledad, who has taken pity upon us!" It brought tears to the eyes of the stoutest veterans to witness this line of unfortunates, reminding us of our mothers, wives, sisters, and daughters. All possible kindness and attention were shown them.

The reaction came very near upsetting two, who became hysterical from over-excitement, and could not be assured that the Chiricahuas were not going to take them away. They did not recover their natural composure until the expedition had crossed the boundary line.

"Hieronymo" had another interview with General Crook, whom he assured he wanted to make a peace to last forever. General Crook replied that "Hieronymo" had waged such bloody war upon our people and the Mexicans that he did not care to let him go back to San Carlos; a howl would be raised against any man who dared to grant terms to an outlaw for whose head two nations clamored. If "Hieronymo" were willing to lay down his arms and go to work at farming, General Crook would allow him to go back; otherwise the best thing he could do would be to remain just where he was and fight it out.

"I am not taking your arms from you," said the General, "because I am not afraid of you with them. You have been allowed to go about camp freely, merely to let you see that we have strength enough to exterminate you if we want to ; and you have seen with your own eyes how many Apaches are fighting on our side and against you. In making peace with the Americans, you must also be understood as making peace with the Mexicans, and also that you are not to be fed in idleness, but set to work at farming or herding, and make your own living."

"Hieronymo," in his reply, made known his contempt for the Mexicans, asserted that he had whipped them every time, and in the last fight with them hadn't lost a man. He would go to the San Carlos with General Crook and work at farming or anything else. All he asked for was fair play. He contended that it was unfair to start back to the San Carlos at that time, when his people were scattered like quail, and when the women and children now in our hands were without food or means of transportation. The old and the little ones could not walk. The Chiricahuas had many ponies and donkeys grazing in the different cañons. Why not remain one week longer? "Loco" and all the other Chiricahuas would then have arrived; all the ponies would be gathered up; a plenty of mescal and pony-meat on hand, and the march could be made securely and safely. But if General Crook left the Sierra Madre, the Mexicans would come in to catch and kill the remnant of the band, with whom "Hieronymo," would cast his fortunes.

General Crook acknowledged the justice of much which "Hieronymo" had said, but declined to take any action not in strict accord with the terms of the convention. He would now move back slowly, so as not to crowd the young and feeble too much ; they should have time to finish roasting mescal, and most of those now out could catch up with the column; but those who did not would have to take the chances of reaching San Carlos in safety.

"Hieronymo" reiterated his desire for peace; said that he himself would start out to gather and bring in the remnants of his people, and he would cause the most diligent search to be made for Charlie McComas. If possible, he would join the Americans before they got out of the Sierra Madre. If not, he would make his way to the San Carlos as soon as this could be done without danger; "but," concluded he, "I will remain here until I have gathered up the last man, woman, and child of the Chiricahuas."

All night long the Chiricahuas and the Apache scouts danced together in sign of peace and good-will. The drums were camp-kettles

7

partly filled with water and covered tightly
with a well-soaked piece of calico. The drum-
sticks were willow saplings curved into a hoop
at one extremity. The beats recorded one hundred to the minute, and were the same dull,
solemn thump which scared Cortés and his
beleagured followers during *la Noche triste.*
No Caucasian would refer to it as music;
nevertheless, it had a fascination all its own
comparable to the whirr-r-r of a rattlesnake.
And so the song, chanted to the measure of the
drumming, had about it a weird harmony which
held listeners spell-bound. When the dance
began, two old hags, white-haired and stiff with
age, pranced in the centre of the ring, warming
up under the stimulus of the chorus until they
became lively as crickets. With them were
two or three naked boys of very tender years.
The ring itself included as many as two hundred Indians of both sexes, whose varied cost-
umes of glittering hues made a strange setting
to the scene as the dancers shuffled and sang
in the silvery rays of the moon and the flicker-
ing light of the camp-fires.

On May 23, 1883, rations were issued to 220

Chiricahuas, and, soon after, Nané, one of the most noted and influential of the Chiricahua chiefs, rode into camp with seventeen of his people. He has a strong face, marked with intelligence, courage, and good nature, but with an under stratum of cruelty and vindictiveness. He has received many wounds in his countless fights with the whites, and limps very perceptibly in one leg. He reported that Chiricahuas were coming in by every trail, and that all would go to the San Carlos as soon as they collected their families.

On the 24th of May the march back to the San Carlos began. All the old Chiricahuas were piled on mules, donkeys, and ponies ; so were the weak little children and feeble women. The great majority streamed along on foot, nearly all wearing garlands of cotton-wood foliage to screen them from the sun. The distance travelled was not great, and camp was made by noon.

The scene at the Bávispe River was wonderfully picturesque. Sit down on this flat rock and feast your eyes upon the silver waves flashing in the sun. Don't scare that little girl who

is about to give her baby brother a much-
needed bath. The little dusky brat—all eyes
—is looking furtively at you and ready to
bawl if you draw nearer. Opposite are two
old crones filling *ollas* (jugs or jars) of basket-
work, rendered fully water-proof by a coating
of either mesquite or piñon pitch. Alongside
of them are two others, who are utilizing the
entrails of a cow for the same purpose. The
splash and yell on your right, as you correctly
divine, come from an Apache "Tom Sawyer,"
who will one day mount the gallows. The
friendly greeting and request for "tobacco
shmoke" are proffered by one of the boys, who
has kindly been eating a big portion of your
meals for several days past, and feels so friendly
toward you that he announces himself in a
pleasant, off-hand sort of way as your *"Sikisn"*
(brother). Behind you are grouped Apache
scouts, whose heads are encircled with red flan-
nel bandages, and whose rifles and cartridges
are never laid aside. Horses and mules plunge
belly-deep into the sparkling current ; soldiers
come and go, some to drink, some to get buck-
ets filled with water, and some to soak neck,

APACHE BASKET WORK.

face, and hands, before going back to din-
ner.

In this camp we remained several days. The
old and young squaws had cut and dried large
packages of " jerked " beef, and had brought
down from the hillsides donkey-loads of mescal
heads, which were piled in ovens of hot stones
covered with wet grass and clay. The process
of roasting, or rather steaming, mescal takes
from three to four days, and resembles somewhat the mode of baking clams in New Eng-
land. The Apache scouts passed the time
agreeably enough in gambling with the Chiricahuas, whom they fleeced unmercifully, win-
ning hundreds of dollars in gold, silver, and
paper at the games of *monte, conquien, tzi-chis*,
and *mushka*.

The attractive pools of the Bávispe wooed
groups of white soldiers and packers, and
nearly the whole strength of the Chiricahua
women and children, who disported in the refreshing waters with the agility and grace of
nereids and tritons. The modesty of the
Apaches of both sexes, under all circumstances,
is praiseworthy.

"Chato" and "Loco" told General Crook this morning that "Hieronymo" had sent them back to say that the Chiricahuas were very much scattered since the fight, and that he had not been as successful as he anticipated in getting them united and in corraling their herds of ponies. They did not want to leave a single one of their people behind, and urged General Crook to stay in his present camp for a week longer, if possible. "Loco," for his part, expressed himself as anxious for peace. He had never wished to leave San Carlos. He wanted to go back there and obtain a little farm, and own cattle and horses, as he once did. Here it may be proper to say that all the chiefs of the Chiricahuas—"Hieronymo," "Loco," "Chato," "Nané," "Bonito," "Chihuahua," "Maugas," "Zelé," and "Kantenné"—are men of noticeable brain power, physically perfect and mentally acute—just the individuals to lead a forlorn hope in the face of every obstacle.

The Chiricahua children, who had become tired of swimming, played at a new sport today, a mimic game of war, a school of practice analogous to that established by old Fagan for the instruction of young London pickpockets. Three boys took the lead, and represented Mexicans, who endeavored to outrun, hide from, or elude their pursuers, who trailed them to their covert, surrounded it, and poured in a flight of arrows. One was left for dead, stretched upon the ground, and the other two were seized and carried into captivity. The fun became very exciting, so much so that the corpse, ignoring the proprieties, raised itself up to see how the battle sped.

In such sports, in such constant exercise, swimming, riding, running up and down the steepest and most slippery mountains, the Apache passes his boyish years. No wonder his bones are of iron, his sinews of wire, his muscles of India-rubber.

On May 27, 1883, the Chiricahuas had finished roasting enough mescal to last them to the San Carlos. One of the Apache scouts came running in very much excited. He told his story to the effect that, while hunting some distance to the north, he had discovered a large body of Mexican soldiers; they were driving back the band of cattle run off by " Hieronymo," and previously referred to. The scout tried to communicate with the Mexicans, who imagined him to be a hostile Indian, and fired three shots at him. Lieutenant Forsyth, Al. Zeiber, and a small detachment of white and Indian soldiers started out to overtake the Mexicans. This they were unable to do, although they went some fifteen miles.

On the 28th, 29th, and 30th of May the march was continued back toward the San Carlos. The rate of progress was very slow, the Mexican captives not being able to ride any great distance along the rough trails, and several of our men being sick. Two of the scouts were so far gone with pneumonia that their death was predicted every hour, in spite of the assurances of the "medicine-men" that their incantations would bring them through all right. "Hieronymo," "Chato," "Kan-tenné,' and "Chihuahua" came back late on the night of the 28th, leading a large body of 116 of their people, making an aggregate of 384 in camp on the 29th.

On the 30th, after a march, quite long under the circumstances,—fifteen to eighteen miles,—

we crossed the main "divide" of the Sierra Madre at an altitude of something over 8,000 feet. The pine timber was large and dense, and much of it on fire, the smoke and heat parching our throats, and blackening our faces.

With this pine grew a little mescal and a respectable amount of the *madroña*, or mountain mahogany. Two or three deer were killed by the Apache scouts, and as many turkeys; trout were visible in all the streams. The line of march was prolific in mineral formations,— basalt, lava, sandstone, granite, and limestone. The day the command descended the Chihuahua side of the range it struck the trail of a large body of Mexican troops, and saw an inscription cut into the bark of a mahogany stating that the Eleventh Battalion had been here on the 21st of May.

The itinerary of the remainder of the homeward march may be greatly condensed. The line of travel lay on the Chihuahua side and close to the summit of the range. The country was extremely rough, cut up with rocky cañons beyond number and ravines of great depth, all flowing with water. Pine forests covered all the elevated ridges, but the cañons and lower foothills had vegetation of a different character: oak, juniper, maple, willow, rose, and blackberry bushes, and strawberry vines. The weather continued almost as previously described,—the days clear and serene, the nights bitter cold, with ice forming in pails and kettles on the 2d and 3d of June. No storms worthy of mention assailed the command, the sharp showers that fell two or three times being welcomed as laying the soot and dust.

Game was found in abundance,—deer and turkey. This the Apache scouts were permitted to shoot and catch, to eke out the rations which had completely failed, the last issue being made June 4th. From that date till June 11th, inclusive, all hands lived upon the country. The Apaches improved the excellent opportunity to show their skill as hunters and their accuracy with fire-arms.

The command was threatened by a great prairie fire on coming down into the broad grassy valley of the Janos. Under the impetus of a fierce wind the flames were rushing upon camp. There was not a moment to be

FIGHTING THE PRAIRIE FIRE.

lost. All hands turned out,—soldiers, scouts, squaws, Chiricahua warriors, and even children. Each bore a branch of willow or cotton-wood, a blanket, or scrap of canvas. The conflagration had already seized the hill-crest nearest our position; brownish and gray clouds poured skyward in compact masses; at their feet a long line of scarlet flame flashed and leaped high in air. It was a grand, a terrible sight: in front was smiling nature, behind, ruin and desolation. The heat created a vacuum, and the air, pouring in, made whirlwinds, which sent the black funnels of soot winding and twisting with the symmetry of hour-glasses almost to the zenith. For one moment the line of fire paused, as if to rest after gaining the hill-top; it was only a moment. "Here she comes!" yelled the men on the left; and like a wild beast flinging high its tawny mane of cloud and flashing its fangs of flame, the fire was upon, around, and about us.

Our people stood bravely up to their work, and the swish! swish! swish! of willow brooms proved that camp was not to be surrendered without a struggle.

We won the day; that is, we saved camp, herds, and a small area of pasturage; but over a vast surface of territory the ruthless flames swept, mantling the land with soot and an opaque pall of mist and smoke through which the sun's rays could not penetrate. Several horses and mules were badly burned, but none to death.

For two or three nights afterwards the horizon was gloriously lighted with lines of fire creeping over the higher ridges. As we debouched into the broad plain, through which trickled the shriveled current of the Janos, no one would have suspected that we were not a column of Bedouins. A long caravan, stretched out for a mile upon the trail, resolved itself upon closer approach into a confused assemblage of ponies, horses, and mules, with bundles or without, but in every case freighted with humanity. Children were packed by twos and threes, while old women and feeble men got along as best they could, now riding, now walking. The scouts had decked themselves with paint and the Chiricahua women had donned all their finery of rough silver bracelets, wooden crosses, and saints' pictures captured from Mexicans. This undulating plain, in which we now found ourselves, spread far to the north and east, and was covered with bunch and grama grasses, and dotted with cedar. The march brought us to Alisos Creek (an affluent of the Janos), a thousand yards or more above the spot where the Mexican commander Garcia, had slaughtered so many Chiricahua women and children. Human bones, picked white and clean by coyotes, glistened in the sandy bed of the stream. Apache baskets and other furniture were strewn about. A clump of graves headed by rude crosses betrayed the severity of the loss inflicted upon the Mexicans.

Between the 5th and 8th of June we crossed back (west) into Sonora, going over the asperous peak known as the Cocospera.

In this vicinity were many varieties of mineral—granite gneiss, porphyry, conglomerate, shale, sandstone, and quartz,—and travel was as difficult almost as it had been in the earlier days of the march. We struck the head waters of Pitisco Creek, in a very rugged cañon, then Elias Creek, going through another fine game region, and lastly, after crossing a broad table-land mantled with grama grass, mesquite, Spanish bayonet, and Palo Verde, mescal, and palmilla, bivouacked on the San Bernardino river, close to a tule swamp of blue, slimy mud.

The scouts plastered their heads with this mud, and dug up the bulbs of the tule, which, when roasted, are quite palatable.

On the 15th of June the command recrossed the national boundary, and reached Silver Springs, Arizona, the camp of the reserve under Colonel Biddle, from whom and from all of whose officers and men we received the warmest conceivable welcome. Every disaster had been predicted and asserted regarding the column, from which no word had come, directly or indirectly since May 5th. The Mexican captives were returned to their own country and the Chiricahuas marched, under Crawford, to the San Carlos Agency.

Unfortunately the papers received at Silver Springs were full of inflammatory telegrams, stating that the intention of the government was to hang all the Chiricahua men, without distinction, and to parcel out the women and children among tribes in the Indian Territory. This news, getting among the Chiricahuas, produced its legitimate result. Several of the chiefs and many of the head men hid back in the mountains until they could learn exactly what was to be their fate. The Mexican troops went in after them, and had two or three severe engagements, and were, of course, whipped each time. When the road was clear the Chiricahuas kept their promises to the letter, and brought to the San Carlos the last man, woman, and child of their people.

They have been quietly scattered in small groups around the reservation, the object being to effect tribal disintegration, to bring individuals and families face to face with the progress made by more peaceable Apaches, and at same time to enable trusted members of the latter bands to maintain a more perfect surveillance over every action of the Chiricahuas.

Charlie McComas was never found; the Chiricahuas insist, and I think truthfully, that he was in the *rancheria* destroyed by Crawford; that he escaped, terror-stricken, to the depths of the mountains; that the country was so rough, the timber and brush-wood so thick that his tracks could not be followed, even had there not been such a violent fall of rain during the succeeding nights. All accounts agree in this.

Altogether the Chiricahuas delivered up thirteen captives,—women and children,—held by them as hostages.